unveiling eternal bliss

Principles of Vedanta, Modern Psychology and Practical Insights For Enduring Happiness

HARSHA RAO

ISBN 979-8-89277-756-8

This book is Dedicated to my Parents

for their selfless love,

the true Karma Yogis

This book would NOT be possible without the

Inspiration from my Wife,

Inquisitiveness from my Teenage Daughter

CONTENTS

FOREWORD

Writing a book was never part of my bucket list!

This book started as a bunch of notes I scribbled in my notebook, absolutely captivated by the enormity of the subject of Vedanta (One of the schools of Hinduism). I am positive there are many of you out there, like me, who are never satisfied with the status quo that is life around us. This journey started two years back, and my preparatory steps were to gain knowledge without judgment. I spent most of my spare time reading books, scriptures, and journals. My sheer passion for this subject made these hours and days of reading appear as no effort at all. It is paramount to realize that there is no end to this learning, nor it should be. Our efforts to learn and assimilate are infinite and endless.

This book is meant to be an introduction and not an in-depth treatise on the subject matter. Hundreds of books have been written on Vedanta by both Indian and Western philosophers and great theologians. This book is not meant to be a replacement for the work done by the innumerable souls in advancing Vedanta. The primary purpose of this book is a guidepost to what is out there, a sort of map of the terrain. I have made modest attempts to assimilate both Eastern and Western viewpoints on the subject of *Vedanta* and its true goal of attaining eternal bliss. Enduring happiness, consciousness, anatomy of the mind, human intellect, and other cognition-related topics are of significant interest to modern psychologists. Due to the mystical nature of this subject, there is fascinating scientific research ongoing in all the major educational institutions across the world. The goal of this research is to attempt to find a harmony between Science and Spirituality.

It has been said that the knowledge of *Sanskrit* (the language in which the *Vedas* and ancient Hindu scriptures were written) might be essential before one learns to read and understand these scriptures. While I agree that reading these scriptures in the language in which they were written has no substitute, I still believe, however, that English or any other language translation can be a substitute for understanding the principles. After all, what we are learning needs to go beyond the senses; more of that will be covered in the book.

Sanskrit words from the scriptures are used throughout this book, and the Sanskrit words are highlighted in Italic font. Wherever possible, a transliteration in English has been given. There is significant power in reading these scriptures aloud, and my hope is that the English transliteration can help with that.

The concept of Vedanta predominantly discussed in this book is the Advaita Vedanta, which highlights the oneness of the individual being and the divinity. This is the school of Vedanta that has personally influenced me enormously, and the universality of monism is critical in a world where religious hatred is rampant. The dualistic Vedanta philosophies have significant value, too. However, they are not covered in-depth in this book, and it is best to discuss them as a separate subject, a separate book perhaps.

I have, however, presented the various schools of Hinduism, which are propounded by the greatest philosophers.

Writing this book has been an absolute joy. I sincerely hope that you will enjoy reading this book as much as I enjoyed writing it.

– Harsha Rao

Nov 13, 2023

PART I – VEDAS & VEDANTA

(ANCIENT & ETERNAL PHILOSOPHY)

Chapter 1

INTRODUCTION

I am not a saint, I am not a monk, I am not a celebrity, I am not rich, I am not famous…

I am just an ordinary man wondering if there's more to life.

Life is filled with a constant whirlwind of emotions ranging from joy, sorrow, anger, envy, lust, greed, fear to name a few. The lens through which we view these emotions also constantly changes as we age. Things that used to bring us great joy when we were young, whether it be eating mangoes, riding a bike, or seeing a color television for the first time, no longer ignite the same joy in us. Something happens to us as we age, and the sense of joy or happiness does not seem enduring or eternal. Most of us just float through life like a feather blown in the direction of the wind. We readily accept the status quo that we call life.

What is the real reason we are born? What do we do or not do to live a purposeful life? What is the real meaning of purpose anyway? Is there a higher truth? Who are we really? Are we just a heap of body and mind?

I have spent four and a half decades of my life living what I unequivocally thought was an amazing life. The transient and impermanent nature of what we call joy really baffled me. Why can't there be permanent bliss for all of us all the time? Is it possible for us to get there?

As Gautama the Buddha said,

सर्वं दुःखं, सर्वं क्षणिकं, सर्वं अनित्यम्

"Sarvam dukham, sarvam kshanikam, sarvam anityam"

"All is suffering, All is impermanent, All is transient"

Is there a way out of this? Are we, as humans, supposed to lead a higher life? How do we get there? What does it feel like when we get there?

As I started introspecting on all of these philosophical questions a bit deeper, I realized that great philosophers and ancient sages have been asking the same questions and have poured their knowledge through teachings and scriptures that have been percolating for thousands of years.

What did they say? Did they make any logical or analytical sense? Do I just have to believe what they said, or can I experience it myself? The cynic in me started asking these questions, and my quest began.

The word bliss or eternal happiness seemed like an abstract concept to me, and I wanted a logical and realizable definition of this state of bliss. The engineer in me started to map the concept of eternal bliss as a two-dimensional graph.

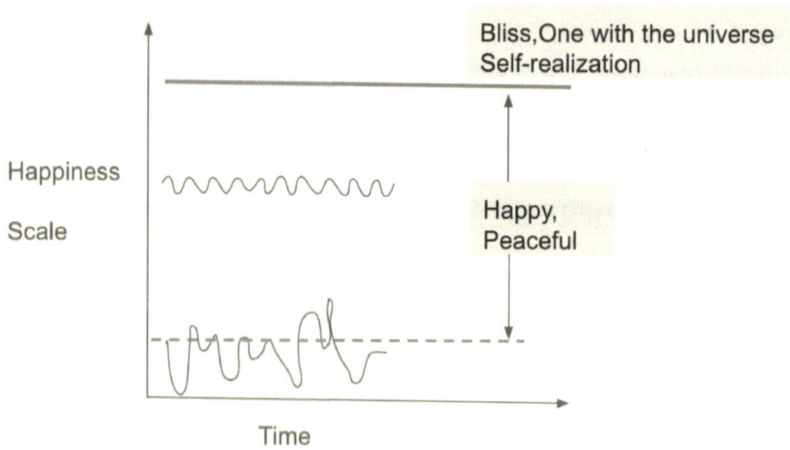

Naturally, all of us are in the lower squiggly graph, happy for just an instant and then moving to our discontented or unhappy state, and the cycle repeats. Even a person with the most basic amount of cognitive knowledge would choose to be in the higher happiness scale all the time. So, the real question is, what prevents us from being in that state, not just as a transient phase but continually? Have you ever wondered why we cannot maintain this state of happiness all the time? What are the triggers that circumvent us from being in this blissful state?

The triggers that prevent us from being in this state of bliss are beautifully described in the Bhagavad Gita (the holiest book in Vedanta and will be covered later):

"ध्यायतो विषयान्पुंसः संगस्तेषूपजायते।
संगात्सञ्जायते कामः कामात्क्रोधोऽभिजायते।।"

"क्रोधाद्भवति सम्मोहः सम्मोहात्स्मृतिविभ्रमः।
स्मृतिभ्रंशाद् बुद्धिनाशो बुद्धिनाशात्प्रणश्यति।।"

*"Dhyayato vishayan pumsah sangas tesupajayate
Sangat sanjayate kamah kamat krodho 'bhijayate"*

*"Krodhad bhavati sammohah sammohat smrti-vibhramah
Smrti-bhramsad buddhi-naso buddhi-nasat pranasyati"*

"While contemplating the objects of the senses, a person develops attachment to them, and from such attachment, lust develops. From lust, anger arises."

"From anger, complete delusion arises, and from delusion, bewilderment of memory. When memory is bewildered, intelligence is lost, and when intelligence is lost, one falls down again into the material pool."

How do we control our senses and the trigger factors that prevent us from being on this higher happiness scale all the time?

Fortunately, there are answers to these hard questions and much more in the treasures of Hindu philosophy called *Vedanta* (which literally means End of the Vedas in Sanskrit). The first of the Vedas was discovered more than 5000 years ago!! We will delve into these in the later chapters. Hindu philosophy, or *Vedanta,* was not new to me. Having been born in a traditional Hindu family, this knowledge was always available to me, but my *Avidya* (Ignorance) to discriminate what's important got the better of me.

This is very similar to the story from Sri Ramakrishna's parable of a washerman who stumbled upon a huge piece of diamond near the river. He just did not know what this shiny piece of rock was, and neither did any of his friends. The washerman used this rock to clean the dirty clothes!! One day, a learned man from another village happened to see the washerman use this pristine diamond to clean clothes; he was awe-struck at the *"avidya"* of the washerman.

Better late than never!! In pursuit of finding a higher truth, I am grateful that the cloud of *Avidya* was lifted to reveal the luminous sun, which is *Vedanta*. My intention is not to preach but to share my experiences that have had a paradigm shift in me and, hence, the life around me. I considered myself to be highly analytical and a strong agnostic when it came to religion.

The essence of *Vedanta* is highly analytical and is all about YOU. There is no objective knowledge but it is all subjective. This interesting juxtaposition has attracted great scientific minds to *Vedanta*, from Nikola Tesla to Schrödinger to Heisenberg to Bohr, to name a few.

I hope the next few chapters that explain the essence of *Vedanta* and its application to daily life will be as life-changing for you as it has been for me, as I am nothing but an ordinary person trying to uncover what is extraordinary within oneself!

The aim of this book is to demystify *Vedanta* to achieve:

Inner peace,

Self-realization,

Pure bliss and

Union with a diviner higher reality.

Vedanta is a pure treasure and is an absolute life-changer if YOU decide to join this journey of **self-discovery.**

This book is organized into four parts that can be read fairly independently of each other. However, it is recommended to follow the flow of the book to get the maximum benefit of the context.

The four parts are chronological in order, with Part I discussing the most ancient material and scriptures and Part IV discussing the individual insights of the author gleaned from the summary of Parts I through III.

Part I of this book is organized into five chapters:

- Chapter 2 discusses the six orthodox schools of Hindu Philosophy, with *Vedanta* being one of them. It is imperative to understand the other schools of thought before we delve into our subject, which is *Vedanta*.

- Chapter 3 delves straight into the history of how and when the Vedas were discovered and what the four key Vedas entail.

- Chapter 4 discusses the high-level teachings of *Vedanta*, including the ten key *Upanishads*. This chapter does not discuss these ten *Upanishads* in detail but rather at a higher-level. The key teachings from these ten *Upanishads* are sprinkled across the entire book. The Upanishads are considered to be the cream of the Vedas and contain Metaphysical, philosophical, and self-realization topics, which are the heart of *Vedanta*.

- Chapter 5 discusses the high-level teachings of the *Bhagavad Gita* (Song of God), the holiest book of Hindu philosophy. Only the second chapter of the Bhagavad Gita is discussed, and the reader is encouraged to explore a wealth of references to read the rest of the chapters.

Part II discusses the fusion of East and Western philosophy, termed Neo Vedanta, which was formulated in mid to late 19th-century India.

Part III discusses the scientific studies in the field of psychology and correlates the findings between what modern science and Hindu

Spirituality have in common with attaining enduring happiness or eternal bliss.

Part IV summarizes the key practical and personal insights the author gleaned from the preceding three parts of the book.

Chapter 2

SCHOOLS OF HINDUISM

Before we delve into the essence of *Vedanta*, it behooves us to understand the history of how all this came about.

Since ancient times, humans have been searching for a rational explanation for the mysteries of creation, life, and existence.

Hinduism is the world's oldest religion, dating back to 2500 BCE, almost 5000 years ago! There are six broad schools of Hindu philosophy that are widely accepted. These are termed the *"Shat Darshana"* (6 systems of philosophy or views).

1. *Nyaya* – This school of philosophy primarily deals with the theory of knowledge and logic. According to the Nyaya school of Hindu philosophy, there are four means to gain knowledge: Perception (*pratyaksha*), Inference (*anumana*), Comparison (*upamana*), and Proof via sound or testimony (*shabda*). This draws great parallels to modern science, and the fact that these *Nyaya Sutras* (texts of Nyaya school) were written thousands of years ago before modern scientific evolution in the West, shines a light on the advanced nature of these philosophies.

2. *Vaisheshika* – This school of philosophy is very similar (although independently developed during the same time) to the Nyaya philosophy and postulates that all objects in the physical universe are made up of super tiny particles called *paramanu* (atoms) and is more metaphysical in its context. This school also projects that one's experiences are the various interactions of this paramanu. The *Vaisheshika* school only accepts Perception

(*Pratyaksha*) and Inference (*Anumana*) as the only reliable means of valid knowledge.

3. *Sankhya (Samkhya)* – This school of philosophy is dualist in nature and proclaims that the world is perceived as comprising two elements: *Purusha* (eternal being) and *Prakriti* (matter). In the Sankhya system, there is no one divine creator; instead, the universe is seen because of various interactions in matter (Prakriti). We won't delve into the depths of Sankhya in this book, as there are some similarities with the Vedanta philosophy which will be explained in future chapters.

    Sankhya means "empirical" or "number" in Sanskrit. According to Sankhya, all of creation stems from the two facets of *Purusha & Prakriti*. *Purusha* is pure consciousness, the soul, Self, or knower. It is not substance but rather essence, beyond time and activity. *Prakriti* is matter and Nature. It is the power of manifestation in all objects.

    Sankhya also believes in three *pramanas* as the means of gaining knowledge: *Pratyaksha* (perception), *Anumana* (inference), and *Shabda* (word/testimony/proof from reliable sources).

    Sankhya is also considered a non-theistic philosophy as it does not propose a personal god or supreme deity who is responsible for the creation of the universe. The primary goal of this philosophy is the liberation of the individual soul (purusha) through self-realization and knowledge.

4. *Yoga* – This philosophy is probably the most well-known in the Western world, but for all the wrong reasons, it is associated with just the physical aspect of yoga postures. The definition of Yoga in Sanskrit really means the union of oneself with the divine.

The Yoga school of philosophy seems to have been significantly based on the Sankhya philosophy, which we briefly discussed earlier. The Yoga school seems to have originated in the 1st century BC, much later than the other Hindu schools of philosophy and is attributed to the great sage Patanjali. Patanjali's Yoga sutras are a collection of aphorisms aimed at giving a concise guide to the practice and philosophy of Yoga.

The Yoga philosophy has some fundamental differences with the Sankhya philosophy.

Sankhya is fundamentally an atheistic philosophy that does not believe in a personal god, while Yoga (*Bhakti* Yoga specifically) propagates surrendering oneself in devotion to a personal god, *Ishvara* (God), to attain liberation.

Sankhya places more emphasis on attaining liberation through knowledge by seeking to discriminate between Purusha and Prakriti, while Yoga places more emphasis on practice, including meditation, concentration, and self-discipline to attain liberation. These Yogic techniques are termed *Ashtanga* (8 steps) and are explained in the next section.

Some scholars (Adi Shankaracharya, more on this later) have termed Yoga philosophy as *Sankhya* with God. The fifth and sixth schools of Hinduism deals with Vedas. The fifth school is called "Purva Mimamsa" (Earlier Enquiry) and the sixth school is called "Uttara Mimamsa" (Later Enquiry). Uttara Mimamsa is also sometimes synonymously used to denote the Vedanta school of Hinduism.

PATANJALI'S YOGA SUTRAS

So, what exactly is *Yoga* according to Patanjali?

The most famous definition of Yoga comes in the Yoga Sutras written by Patanjali (Verse two of the 1st chapter):

I.2 योगश्चित्तवृत्तिनिरोधः
yogaś citta-vṛtti-nirodhaḥ

Yoga is the cessation of the patterns (*Vritti*) of consciousness (*Citta*).

This definitely needs some explanation.

Yoga – This refers to the practice and discipline of Yoga, which will be explained in the next chapter (Ashtanga Yoga). The aim of this is to achieve inner peace, self-realization, and union with a diviner of higher reality.

Citta – The whole gamut of consciousness which includes thoughts, emotions, and mental activities.

Vritti – Modifications or fluctuations of the activities in the mind, including thoughts, desires, and distractions.

Nirodhah – Cessation, control, restrain.

In essence, according to Patanjali, one can attain supreme inner peace if one can transcend the ordinary fluctuations of the mind. The means to attaining that is explained in the Ashtanga Yoga Sutras.

ASHTANGA YOGA SUTRAS

The great sage Patanjali goes on to explain the Ashtanga (8 limbs in Sanskrit) to achieve supreme transcendental bliss or liberation.

These are explained in Chapter 2 of the Patanjali Yoga Sutras.

II.29 यमनियमासनप्राणायामप्रत्याहारधारणाध्यानसमाधयोऽष्टावङ्गानि

yama-niyamāsana-prāṇāyāma-pratyāhāra-dhāraṇā-dhyāna-samādhayo ʻṣṭāv aṅgāni

The eight components of the Yoga system are:
1. Yama – External discipline or ethical principles
2. Niyama – Internal or personal discipline
3. Asana – Posture
4. Pranayama – Regulation of Breath
5. Pratyahara – Withdrawal of the senses
6. Dharana – Concentration
7. Dhyana – Meditation
8. Samadhi – Oneness, integration

These eight limbs are characterized by many scholars as a step-by-step ladder, as illustrated in the next visual. Each limb builds upon the previous one. It is only logical that the seeker of liberation needs to have the basic tenets of Yama and Niyama (ethical internal and external disciplines). It is not possible to bypass any of these steps to get right to Samadhi, which is explained as oneness with the universe.

We will discuss the concept of oneness when we delve into the main subject of this book, Vedanta, in later chapters.

Patanjali further explains that there are five yamas (external disciplines) needed as the first step in attaining self-realization.

II.30 अहिंसासत्यास्तेयब्रह्मचर्यापरिग्रहा यमाः

ahimsā-satyāsteya-brahmacaryāparigrahā yamāḥ

The five tenets of ethics (yama) are:

Ahimsa – not harming

Satya – Truthfulness

Asteya – Not stealing

Brahmacharya – chastity, impeccable conduct

Aparigraha – non-possessiveness

Patanjali also adds another five *niyamas* (internal disciplines).

II.32 शौचसन्तोषतपःस्वाध्यायेश्वरप्रणिधानानि नियमाः

śauca-santoṣa-tapaḥ-svādhyāyeśvara-praṇidhānāni niyamāḥ

These five internal disciplines are:

Sauca – purity

Santosa – contentment

Tapah – austerity (intensity of discipline)

Svadhyaya – self-study

Isvara Pranidhana – Surrender in pure devotion to Isvara (personal God)

There are significant similarities between yama and niyamas to the ten commandments in Judeo-Christian philosophy.

"You shall not murder"

"You shall not bear false witness"

"You shall not steal"

"You shall not covet"

These are some examples that relate well to the ethical principles and internal discipline that all of us need to have before seeking liberation or aiming for a life of infinite bliss.

The third limb, once the seeker has attained all the internal and external disciplines, is called *Asana* (or posture). This also does not have any relevance to the yoga gyms we see all over today. The real purpose of asana is for the seeker to sit comfortably for a longer time without getting disturbed. As explained by Patanjali in yoga sutras,

II.46 स्थिरसुखमासनम्
sthira-sukham āsanam

The postures should embody steadiness and ease to prepare oneself for meditation. You don't have to learn complicated downward dog or any other postures for this. All you need to be able to do is sit comfortably without moving.

Ancient Indian *rsis* and *yogis* sat on a mat or a wooden plank on the ground. The most common yogic sitting position is called *Sukhasana* (happy posture), as illustrated below. The key is to keep your spine straight. Postures have a profound effect on our daily life. We tend to droop when we sit, stand or drive. Changing the position to spine erect will create an instant change in your mood and energy.

The fourth limb of Ashtanga is called *Pranayama* (the practice of breath regulation). Once the seeker has settled in a comfortable *asana*, it is time to focus attention on the breath.

II.49 तस्मिन् सति श्वासप्रश्वासयोर्गतिविच्छेदः प्राणायामः
tasmin sati śvāsa-praśvāsayor gati-vicchedaḥ prāṇāyāmaḥ

Once a steady *asana* is reached, inhalation and exhalation can be regulated, and this is called *pranayama* (breath regulation).

This book does not cover the details of the pranayama approach, which is discussed very elegantly in the analysis of Patanjali's yoga sutras by Swami Vivekananda.

Once close attention is paid to inhalation, storing the breath in the lungs, and exhalation, breath becomes subtle. The distinction between breathing in and breathing out fades away, and the veil lifts from the mind's luminosity, getting it ready for concentration, as explained in the *sutra* below.

II.52 ततः क्षीयते प्रकाशावरणम्
tataḥ kṣīyate prakāśāvaraṇam

"then the veil lifts from the mind's luminosity"

The mind is now ready to concentrate.

The fifth limb of Ashtanga yoga is called Pratyahara (*withdrawal of the senses*). In Chapter 1, we saw a quote from the *Bhagavad Gita* that mentions how senses can lead to attachment and eventual delusion. Patanjali explains that once the mind is ready to concentrate through Pranayama (breath regulation), the realization of external objects fades, and there will be a withdrawal of senses, which is called *Pratyahara*.

II.54 स्वविषयासम्प्रयोगे चित्तस्य स्वरूपानुकार इवेन्द्रियाणां प्रत्याहारः
sva-viṣayāsamprayoge cittasya svarūpānukāra ivendriyāṇām pratyāhāraḥ

"When consciousness interiorizes by uncoupling from external objects, sense withdrawal happens, and that is called *Pratyahara*."

II.55 ततः परमा वश्यतेन्द्रियाणाम्
tataḥ paramā vaśyatendriyāṇām

"Then the senses reside only for the realization of the self."

The first five limbs of *Ashtanga* (yama, niyama, asana, pranayama, and pratyahara) are more external in nature. The last three limbs of *Ashtanga* are internal and are considered very hard, requiring significant practice to achieve and realize. Limb 6 is called *Dharana* (concentration) and is the ability of the *citta* (consciousness) to lock onto a single area. This could be concentrating on things in the body or outside the body. Our citta (mind) is going through so many vrittis (modifications). We are thinking of something constantly, and never is our mind fixated on one thing. The goal of *Dharana* is to fix the mind on one thing. This is one of the hardest things to do and takes significant practice and a spiritual mentality.

III.1 देशबन्धश्चित्तस्य धारणा
deśa-bandhaś cittasya dhāraṇā

"Dharana (concentration) locks consciousness onto a single object."

As an example, if you are concentrating on one thing without any *vrittis* from anywhere else for 12 minutes or more, you are in *Dharana*.

Limb 7 is Dhyana (Meditation).

III.2 तत्र प्रत्ययैकतानता ध्यानम्

tatra pratyayaika-tānatā dhyānam

"An unbroken flow of knowledge to that object is called Dhyana (Meditation)."

According to Swami Vivekananda, *the mind tries to think of one object, to hold itself to one particular spot, such as the top of the head, the heart, etc., and if the mind succeeds in receiving sensations only through that part of the body, and through no other part, that would be Dharana. When the mind succeeds in keeping itself in that state for some time, it is called Dhyana (meditation).*

In essence, *Dhyana* (Meditation) is maintaining Dharana (concentration) for a longer phase.

Limb 8 and the last limb of the Ashtanga is samadhi (integration, bliss) and is subtler than *dharana* and *dhyana*.

III.3 तदेवार्थमात्रनिर्भासं स्वरूपशून्यमिव समाधिः

tad evārtha-mātra-nirbhāsam svarūpa-śūnyam iva samādhiḥ

"When only the essential nature of the object remains as if its formless, pure integration (samadhi) has happened."

And again, Swami Vivekananda says beautifully:

"That is, when in meditation all forms are given up. Suppose I were meditating on a book, and that I have gradually succeeded in concentrating the mind on it, and perceiving only the internal sensations, the meaning, unexpressed in any form, that state of Dhyana is called Samadhi"

Samadhi is said to be a state of pure bliss and the ultimate goal of self-realization. This is the highest state on the chart depicted in Chapter 1.

According to the renowned spiritual master Swami Yogananda Paramahamsa:

"*Samadhi* is the state of Superconsciousness, in which the meditator perceives the identity of the individualized soul and Spirit, as in deep sleep, but is conscious of the united state. *Samadhi* is a high state of spiritual ecstasy – the soul's contact with God. *Samadhi* is known to Yogis as the state of God-Union."

Needless to say, attaining this state of samadhi is immensely hard and requires significant discipline to ascend the *Ashtanga* (eight limbs).

Even though Yoga philosophy by Patanjali is a great gift to mankind for achieving self-realization through practical approaches, it lacks the theistic, philosophical, metaphysical, and scriptural references that *Vedanta* philosophy entails.

Chapter 3

VEDAS

HISTORY

Vedanta (Sanskrit compound word) consists of two words

Veda comes from the Sanskrit root word "Vid," which means "to know" or "knowledge."

Anta means "end," "conclusion," or "culmination."

Vedanta literally means "end of the *Vedas*," "conclusion of the *Vedas*," or "culmination of the *Vedas*."

Vedas refer to the ancient, revered religious scriptures of Hinduism. The exact time period of the origin of the Vedas is unknown. The origin of *Vedas* is attributed to rsis (great sages and scholars), who came out of a deep meditative state and revealed profound teachings to their disciples. Vedas are also classified as shruti, which translates to "that which is heard." These are meant to be the words of the divine and are eternal, not attributed to any one author or *rsi*. Vedas are thus considered to be the most authoritative and foundational texts in Hinduism. Vedas are also termed *Apauruseya* (not attributed to any human origin), further highlighting the divinity of these texts.

To complement this, Hindu philosophy also entails sacred texts called *Smriti* (that which is remembered), which are attributed to human authorship and hence generally do not usurp the authority of the *Vedas*. Smritis are further classified into:

- *Itihasa* (Historical Epics like Ramayana and Mahabharata)

- *Puranas* (Mythological and cosmological stories)

There are a few more classifications of the *Smritis* which are left out for brevity.

During approximately 1500 BCE (almost 4000 years ago), the first written manuscripts of the Vedas started to appear, indicating that the origin of these Vedas must be way before that. *Vedas* are the oldest religious and philosophical sacred texts in the world.

One other unique thing about the Vedas is that they were never written down initially. They were passed orally from the spiritual master (*guru*) to the disciple (*shishya*) for generations. The focus was on the right pronunciation and intonation to maintain the sanctity of these verses. The accurate preservation of the Vedas over centuries could be attributed to the oral nature of transmission. Sometime between 1500 and 1200 BCE, the process of writing down these scriptural verses happened on palm leaves in an ancient *Brahmi* script. It is believed that due to the volume of the Vedas, these codifications as written scriptures happened gradually over centuries. An example of one of the manuscripts written is shown below.

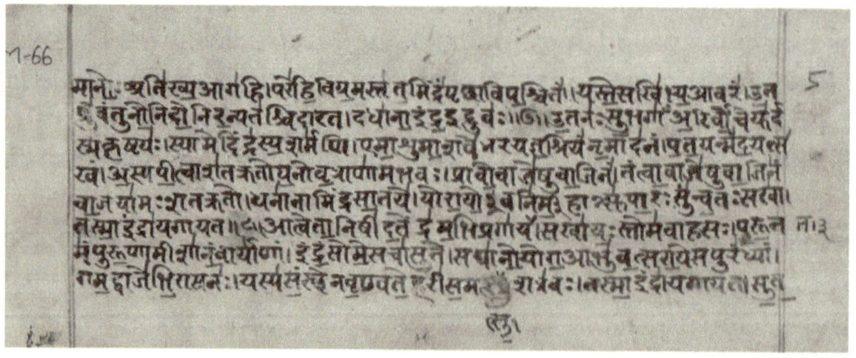

Vedas cannot be attributed to a specific *rsi* (sage or scholar). This points to the selfless nature of these illumined rsis whose main aim was the transmission of this priceless knowledge to their disciples.

It is believed that the first of the Vedas seems to have been written in what is now northwest India (Punjab) in the Indian subcontinent.

CLASSIFICATION OF THE VEDAS

Due to the divine revelations (*shruti*) and the characteristic of being 'not of human origin' (*apauraseya*) of the *Vedas*, there was no general classification of these texts, making it harder for generations of spiritual seekers to understand these very complex texts. Ancient Indian scholars then organized these texts to make it easy for disciples to follow a logical pattern of learning.

The classification of these Vedas is primarily attributed to the great sage *Vyasa*. *Vyasa* is also credited with composing several smritis, including the Mahabharata and Puranas. The holiest Hindu religious book, the *Bhagavad Gita* (song of God), is also part of Mahabharata.

Vedas are divided into four main collections, and we will delve into the details of this in further sections:

1. Rig Veda
2. Yajur Veda
3. Sama Veda
4. Atharva Veda

Furthermore, each of these Vedas is subclassified into four major text types:

- *Samhitas* (Opening verses of the Vedas containing collections of hymns and prayers)

- Each of the Vedas has its own Samhitas at the beginning: *Rig Veda Samhita, Yajur Veda Samhita, Sama Veda Samhita*, and *Atharva Veda Samhita.*

- *Brahmanas* (Follows the *Samhitas* and typically contains details of the rituals and ceremonies)

- *Aranyakas* (Follows the *Brahmanas* and are considered a bridge between the more ritualistic and the philosophical sections of the *Vedas*)

- **Upanishads** (The concluding part of the Vedic literature and hence termed *Vedanta* – "End of the Vedas", containing deep philosophical inquiries into the self, the nature of existence, and the ultimate reality or God-realization)

Upanishads are the crown jewel of the Vedas and encapsulate the highest philosophical teachings and foundations of Hindu philosophy. Due to the supreme brevity of the verses and the need to unpack these to be understandable by spiritual seekers, highly illumined Indian philosophers and spiritual *gurus* have written beautiful commentaries (*bhashya*) on the Upanishads. These will be briefly covered in Chapter 7.

Most of this book only delves into *Vedanta* or the *Upanishads* as a guidepost to lead a purposeful life and move toward self-realization.

The next few sections briefly discuss the Vedas before delving into Vedanta or Upanishads.

RIG VEDA (OLDEST OF THE VEDAS, 1500 BCE AND OLDER):

Rig in Sanskrit means "to praise." These Vedas contain a collection of hymns/poems dedicated to various forces of nature (fire, water, air, etc.), metaphysics, and the creation of the universe. They are among the most profound and earliest spiritual literatures in human existence.

Various Indian and Western minds have fallen deeply in awe with the Rig Veda.

1. Max Müller (German-born philologist and Orientalist): "The Rigveda is the most ancient book in the library of mankind. The study of the Rigveda is the surest way to the knowledge of the ancient world."

2. Sri Aurobindo (Indian philosopher, yogi, and poet): "The Veda is the greatest privilege of this century and of many centuries to come. The Veda is the mother of Indian spiritual culture."

3. Swami Vivekananda (Indian Hindu monk and philosopher): "The Rigveda is the source of all other knowledge which exists, whether Vedanta, Yoga, or Sankhya."

4. A.C. Bhaktivedanta Swami Prabhupada (Founder of the International Society for Krishna Consciousness): "The Rigveda is

the oldest known book of knowledge in the world. It is a perfect and complete system of knowledge."

5. Mahatma Gandhi (Indian independence leader): "The Rigveda is not only for Hindus, but it is for the world."

The Rig Veda is the largest of the four Vedas and is organized into ten *mandalas* (Books). Each *mandala* is subclassified into *Suktas* (hymns), and each *sukta* contains a number of *shlokas* (verses). The *shlokas* are carefully delivered in a very poetic fashion loaded with pristine grammatical purity in Sanskrit. Perfect pronunciation and phonetic connotation are critical, and when uttered correctly, they have a magical significance.

Rigveda has 1028 hymns and is subdivided into 10,600 verses, which shows the enormity of this magnificent philosophical and spiritual gift to mankind.

Most of the *mandalas* contain hymns dedicated to various deities and forces of nature and end with philosophical concepts.

While all *mandalas* are highly significant and have different themes, gods, and purposes, the 10th and the last Mandala of the Rig Veda is considered profound. This Mandala entails philosophical, metaphysical concepts and discusses the concept of **Brahman** representing the **ultimate, formless**, and **infinite** reality.

In the tenth mandala, two *suktas* have special significance:

♦ *Purusha Sukta* (10th Mandala – Hymn 90)

♦ *Nasadiya Sukta* (10th Mandala – Hymn 129)

PURUSHA SUKTAM:

One of the most famous *suktas* (collection of verses) in the Rig Veda is the *Purusha Sukta*. This is the ONLY sukta present in all four Vedas, and hence has supremely high significance. This *sukta* talks about the Purusha (supreme self). The opening verse goes like this:

सहस्रशीर्षा पुरुषः सहस्राक्षः सहस्रपात्।

"Purusha is described as the all-pervading, all-encompassing with thousand heads – thousand eyes and thousand foot"

The number thousand is poetically & metaphorically used to denote the omnipresence of the Purusha or the supreme self. The next few verses describe that he transcends all dimensions.

This *Purusha* is an all-pervading reality that is

- ◆ Immanent (present within the physical world and accessible to human experience in this universe)

- ◆ Transcendent (extending beyond the limitations of the physical world and beyond human experiences)

This points to a formless, infinite and omnipresent aspect of the ultimate reality.

Perhaps the most significant verse in this *sukta* is the following:

वेदाहमेतं पुरुषं महान्तम् ।

आदित्यवर्णंतमसःपरंस्तात् ।

तमेवं विद्वानमृतं इ ह भंवति ।

Vedahametam Purusha mahantam, aditya varnam tamasa parastaat.

Tam eva vidvan, amrutam iha bhavati

"I have known that Supreme *Purusha*, brilliant like the Sun, beyond all darkness. One who knows him, transcends death and reaches Immortality"

This verse highlights that the ultimate reality can be experienced by **you** and that immortality is **here** and **now**, not something in a different world or different life, contrary to other theistic religious beliefs.

Nasadiya Suktam (Hymn of Creation)

This sukta contemplates the mystery of creation and provokes the listener into a deeper inquiry into the creation of the universe, highlighting the significance of intellectual exploration and curiosity.

Several Western philosophers and some contemporary Indian philosophers have equated the *Nasadiya sukta* to the earliest explanation of the Big Bang theory (propagated in the early 1920s). The mere fact that thousands of years ago, illumined rsis could contemplate such a complex metaphysical and cosmological phenomenon highlights the divinity and almost mysticism in these texts.

Nasadiya sukta does not say that God made this universe; on the contrary, it asks how anyone could know how and when the creation happened, as all the gods would have manifested after the creation of the universe. This highlights the highly rational and almost scientific way of the spiritual belief system that is the basis of the Vedic system.

The first *shloka* of the *Nasadiya sukta* begins with an honest inquiry into the creation. The first shloka also highlights the parallelism to the Big Bang theory, where the universe began as a singularity, as an extremely dense and hot point, as explained in the verses below. The third verse highlights that cosmic water (space plasma) is a metaphorical singular entity that existed before the creation of the universe.

According to experts, the usage of "water" is metaphorical and symbolic to define a formless, indistinct, void state before the creation.

नासंदासीन्नो सदांसीत्तदानीम् नासीद्रजो नो व्यौमा पुरो यत्।
किमावरीवु: कुह कस्य शर्मन्नंभ: किमांसीद्रहनं गभीरम्॥१॥
naasadaa-siinno sadaa-siit tadaaniim naasiidrajo no vy-o-maa paro yat |
kimaavariivah kuha kasya sharmannambhah kim-aa-siidgahanam gabhiiram ||1||
There was neither existence nor non-existence, neither matter nor space
What covered it? Where was it? What was its purpose? What protected it? Who was the master of
the cosmic water (space plasma) that was dense and deep?

को अद्धा वेद क इह प्र वोचत्कुत आजाता कुत इयं विसृष्टि:।
अर्वाग्देवा अस्य विसर्जनेनाथा को वेद यत आबभूव॥६॥

ko addhaa v-e-da ka iha pra v-o-chatkuta aaj-aa-taa kuta iyam visrushtihi |
arvaagdevaa asya visarjanenaathaa ko v-e-da yata aababhuuvaa ||6 ||

Who can say and know where all this came from and how all this came to be?
The 'devas' ('gods') came after all this manifested so who knows where all this came from?

इयं विसृष्टिर्यत आबभूव यदि वा दधे यदि वा न।
यो अस्याध्यक्ष: परमे व्योमन्त्सो अङ्ग वेद यदि वा न वेद॥ ७॥

iyam visrushtir-yata aabhabhuuva yadi vaa dadhe yadi va na |
yo asyaadhyakshah parame vy-o-mantso anga ve-eda yadi va ne veda || 7 ||

Where did creation have its origin? Who is One that created it or did the One not create it?
That One alone perceives all from above and knows the beginning or maybe doesn't?

The last two verses highlight the unknown nature of the creation.

न मृत्युरासीदमृतं न तर्हि न रात्र्या अह्न आसीत्प्रकेत:।
आनीदवातं स्वधया तदेकं तस्मांद्धान्यन पर: किंच्चनास॥२॥

na mrutyur-aa-siidamritam na tarhi na raatryaa annha-aasiit praketaha |
aan-ii-davaatam svadhayaa tadekan-tasm-aa-ddhaanyanna parah-kinchanaasa ||2||

There was neither death nor immortality and nothing to separate night and day,
That One existed enclosed in nothingness, there was only that One and no other.

तर्म आसीत्तर्मसा गूळ्हमग्रैंऽप्रकेतं सलिलं सर्वमा इदं।
तुच्छ्येनाभ्वपिहितं यदासीत्तपंसस्तन्मंहिना जांयतैकं॥ ३॥

tama aasiit tamasaa guuL hamagre-e'praketam salilam sarvamaa idam |
tuchhyenaabh-vapihitam -yadaasiit-tapasastan-mahinaa jaa-yataikam-m || 3 ||

Darkness covered darkness, all this was hidden intelligence in cosmic water (Space Plasma)
And the One enclosed in nothing arose from the power of heat.

YAJURVEDA (BETWEEN 1200 AND 800 BC)

We now move on to *YajurVeda*, which is believed to have been developed after the *Rigveda*. Due to the shruti nature of the *YajurVeda* (just like the *Rigveda*), it is hard to depict the exact date of origin. *YajurVeda* borrows heavily from the Rig Veda, and in fact, about 25% of the YajurVeda is found in the *Rigveda*.

Yajur in Sanskrit means "worship," and YajurVeda predominantly deals with the details of the rituals and sacrifices first described in the Rig Veda. YajurVeda provides deep insight into the religious and intellectual components of ancient India. The *Yajurveda* contains *shlokas* or *mantras* (verses) used by ancient Indian rsis (priests/sages) during rituals used to invoke divine energy and highlights the importance these rituals had to connect the material world and the spiritual world.

So, what exactly is this ritual or sacrifice (*yajna*)? Famed Indian theologian and philosopher Sri Aurobindo says, "The elements of the outer sacrifice in the Veda are used as symbols of the inner sacrifice and self-offering; we give what we are and what we have in order that the riches of the Divine Truth and Light may descend into our life and become the elements of our inner birth into the Truth."

"We also make that journey with *Agni* (Fire), the inner flame, as our pathfinder."

The equanimity in lighting the fire for sacrifices to invoke the divine and sacrificing the *Agni* (Fire) within us is profoundly powerful.

One unique thing about *YajurVeda* is the categorization into two main divisions.

Shukla (white/Bright) *Yajurveda* – Characterized by well-organized and comprehensive verses with *Samhitas* (mantras) separated clearly with *Brahmanas* (philosophical teachings) to make it easier for the seeker to analyze.

Krishna (black/dark) *Yajurveda* – A bit more complex with the intertwining of the *Samhitas* (mantras) and Brahmanas (philosophical teachings).

The concluding part of the Yajurveda, also known as the *Upanishads* (*Vedanta*), has highly consequential teachings, and four of them will be studied in detail in the chapter on Vedanta.

Samaveda (same time period as the Rigveda)

The word *"sama"* in Sanskrit means "melody," and there are other meanings of the same word that indicate "harmony" or "balance."

Samaveda is a unique veda that distills the essence of *Rigveda* in a melodic format that is apt for singing in specific tones. The hymns (mantras) of the *Samaveda* are designed to be sung in specific tones during the Vedic rituals. Samaveda is also termed the Veda of melodies by many philosophers. Most of the 1875 verses in Samaveda have been taken from the Rigveda. Samaveda is the shortest of the Vedas.

Samaveda occupies a very special position among all the Vedas, as it is one of the Vedas that Lord Sri *Krishna* compared to himself in the *Bhagavad Gita* (the holiest book of the Hindus). We will spend a considerable amount of time on the teachings in the *Bhagavad Gita* in the later chapters on *Vedanta*.

वेदानां सामवेदोऽस्मि देवानामस्मि वासव: ।

इंद्रियाणां मनश्चास्मि भूतानामस्मि चेतना ॥

vedānāṁ sāma-vedo 'smi devānām asmi vāsavaḥ

indriyāṇām manaś cāsmi bhūtānām asmi cetanā

"I am the Sama Veda among the Vedas; I am Indra among the gods; I am the mind among the senses; and I am consciousness in living beings."

The musical nature of the Samaveda gave birth to Indian classical music. The Samaveda is also considered the earliest known musical notation system in the world. Samaveda gave birth to concepts called *svaras* (musical tones) that Indian classical music adopted gleefully and evolved into various melodic frameworks (*ragas*) and rhythmic tones (*talas*).

The latter portion of the *Samaveda*, called *Upanishads*, contains deep philosophical teachings and forms two significant Upanishads, which we will be discussing later in the chapter on Vedanta.

ATHARVA VEDA (A BIT LATER THAN ALL THE THREE VEDAS)

The meaning of "Atharva" in Sanskrit is not as straightforward as the other three Vedas. There are at least three etymological interpretations of the meaning "Atharva":

♦ Named after the ancient sage Atharva, who is thought to have composed this Veda.

♦ Atharva can also be interpreted as "Practical knowledge," highlighting the diverse range of content in this Veda that is more practical, dealing with healing, medicine, protection, and daily life concerns.

♦ The most etymologically accurate meaning for Atharva is derived from "Athar," which can mean "priest" or "priestly knowledge." This highlights the ritualistic portion (which is still present) in the Atharvaveda.

For the purposes of this book, the "Practical Knowledge" portion makes the most sense as it clearly highlights that this Veda is a bit of a departure from the earlier Vedas. The Atharvaveda themes and subjects are a bit different than the three previous Vedas, as they deal with:

♦ Healing and Medicine: There are numerous hymns related to healing diseases and medicinal plants and herbs. The ancient Indian medicinal system called Ayurveda (which is still used in modern days) originates from the Atharvaveda.

♦ Spells & Charms: Various spells and incantations to help with everyday life's problems make-up some portion of the Atharvaveda.

♦ Social and domestic rituals associated with birth, marriage, death, and coronation are also described in the *Atharvaveda*.

The *Atharvaveda* contains about 730 hymns, making up 6000 mantras. About 1/6th of the Atharvaveda is derived directly from the Rig Veda and most notably from the 10th mandala (story) of the Rigveda.

As is customary in all Vedas, the concluding portion includes philosophical and spiritual teachings called Upanishads, which are part of *Vedanta*. There are three highly significant *Upanishads* in the *Atharvaveda,* which will be discussed in the Vedanta chapter.

VEDAS – CONCLUSION

Some of the key concepts we discussed are highlighted below:

- Vedas are the oldest spiritual books in the history of the world.

- Vedas represent eternal truth revealed by GOD to the great ancient Indian Rsis (sages) in a deep state of meditation.

- All other religions in the world claim authority as being delivered by a special messenger of GOD to certain holy spiritual heads, Vedas do not owe their authority to anyone.

- Vedas themselves are the authority and are eternal.

- Vedas were never written, never created, and are not the utterances of any persons.

- Vedas are not compositions of the human mind.

- The Upanishads (concluding portion) are the most important portion and contain the knowledge and philosophy that forms the basis of Vedanta, which is the pillar of Hinduism.

A NATURAL QUESTION ARISES:

If *Upanishads* are the key essence, then why did the Vedas contain Samhitas (prayers, hymns), *Brahmanas* (sacrificial rituals), *Aranyakas* (philosophical interpretations of the rituals)? What's the point of all these additional texts?

Eminent scholars and philosophers have addressed this very question by dividing the composition of the Vedas into three logical parts to invoke the union with the supreme reality:

- Action (*Karma Kanda*)

  - *Samhitas* & *Brahmanas* are action-oriented.

- Devotion & Meditation (*Upasana Kanda*)

  - *Aranyakas* are more devotion and meditation-focused.

- Knowledge (*Jnana Kanda*)

  - *Upanishads* (part of Vedanta) are more focused on knowledge, philosophical inquiry, and realizing the ultimate truth and attaining spiritual liberation.

These are illustrated in the visual below

Classification of the *Vedas*

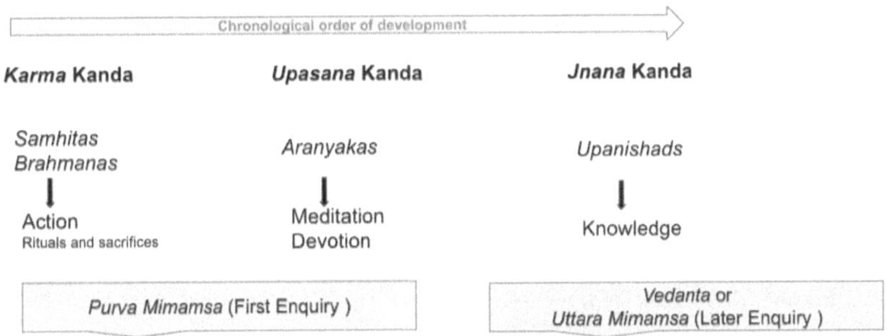

Vedas highlight in a very powerful way that attaining the supreme reality or god.

Vedas highlight in a very powerful way that attaining the supreme reality or God-realization or self-realization involves Action, Devotion, Meditation, and Knowledge. We will unpack these more in the coming chapters.

Chapter 4

VEDANTA

The previous chapter on the introduction to the Vedas highlighted that the crown jewel of the Hindu philosophical system is Vedanta, which is the primary subject matter of this book.

Etymologically, Vedanta means "end of the Vedas," "conclusion of the Vedas," or "culmination of the Vedas."

The word "Vedanta" itself has so much significance that the literal meaning fails to convey the true essence. The essence of the profound philosophical teachings of the *Vedas* has been poured into the *Vedantas*. It can also be construed since these are the culminations; there's nothing beyond them. It's the ultimate truth. It's the final destination!!

Vedanta typically refers to profound cosmic, metaphysical, and spiritual insights found in the *Upanishads*, which are typically (but not always) the concluding portion of the Vedas. Think of these as the summary or conclusion of a long book you have read. All the key essences of the *Vedas* are captured in the *Upanishads* (we will delve into the etymological details of the *Upanishads* later).

Upanishads (between 600 and 300 BC)

Etymologically, the word *Upanishad* is derived from three Sanskrit root words.

Upa: "Near"

Ni: "Down"

Shad: "Sit"

The traditional definition is that *Upanishads* are typically taught when sitting near a guru (spiritual teacher). This emphasizes the importance of acquiring deep spiritual knowledge through direct and close interaction with a teacher. Several other non-etymological definitions of the *Upanishads* are offered, with the prominent one being "Removing ignorance by revealing the knowledge of the supreme spirit."

The *Upanishads* form the philosophical and spiritual core of Hindu philosophy and are the heart of *Vedanta,* dealing with philosophy, consciousness, meditation, self-realization, and god-realization.

Upanishads fundamentally deal with the interconnectedness of

Atman (self) and *Brahman* (ultimate reality)

The Vedanta philosophy is foundationally made up of three authoritative scriptures. It is called *Prasthanatrayi* (the three key sources).

- *Upanishads*

- *Bhagavad Gita (the holy book of Hindu philosophy based on the Upanishads)*

- *Brahma Sutras (Systematic Summary of the Philosophies of the Upanishads)*

We will dedicate this chapter to the Upanishads and delve into the *Bhagavad Gita* and *Brahma Sutras* in subsequent chapters.

Historians estimate that around 108 *Upanishads* are known, and the first thirteen of them are the oldest and are considered to be important. They are termed *"Mukhya"* Upanishads (Principal Upanishads). There are two primary reasons why only the thirteen Upanishads are considered principal.

1. All the major founders of various Vedanta schools of thought wrote extensive commentaries on these 13 Upanishads.

2. All the other "minor" *Upanishads* borrow most of the teachings from these *Mukhya* Upanishads.

Impact of the *Upanishads* on Western Philosophy

Owing to the significance of the teachings in the Upanishads, they were translated into various languages, beginning with Persian as early as the 16th century and French, Latin, English, and German in the early to late nineteenth century.

Some of the profound impact the Upanishads had on Western philosophers can be summed up in their own words.

German philosopher Arthur Schopenhauer:

"In the whole world, there is no study so beneficial and elevating as that of the Upanishads. It has been the solace of my life; it will be the solace of my death."

Austrian physicist Erwin Schrodinger:

"There is obviously only one alternative, namely the unification of minds or consciousnesses. Their multiplicity is only apparent; in truth, there is only one mind. This is the doctrine of the Upanishads."

American essayist and poet Ralph Waldo Emerson:

"Reading the Upanishads is like receiving the sound of the waves into the ear or gazing at the sky or at the stars. It elevates the mind and gives a sense of grandeur."

"The Upanishads contain the essence of Indian wisdom. This essence is here couched in language of unequaled beauty and expression."

"In the morning, I bathe my intellect in the stupendous and cosmogonal philosophy of the Bhagavad Gita, in comparison with which our modern world and its literature seem puny and trivial."

German philosopher and scholar Max Mueller:

"The Upanishads are records of spiritual intuition; texts that offer insight into the nature of ultimate reality, the self, and the universe."

"The Upanishads present the intellectual and philosophical heart of Hinduism, emphasizing the search for spiritual truth and the essence of divinity."

In this book, we will highlight these 13 *Mukhya* (main) Upanishads. So, what are they?

Principal (*Mukhya*) Upanishads

The thirteen principal Upanishads are

Mukhya Upanishads (Principal)

RigVeda	*Yajurveda*	*Samaveda*	*Atharvaveda*
Aitareya	Taittiriya (K)	Chandogya	Mundaka
Kaushitaki	Katha (K)	Kena	Mandukya
	Svetasvatara(K)		Prasna
	Maitri (K)		
	Brihadaranyaka (S)		
	Isha (S)		

Of these thirteen, ten Upanishads (highlighted in light color) are believed to be of the highest essence. The *Upanishads* belonging to *Yajurveda* are highlighted as K or S (belonging to *Krishna* or *Shukla* Yajurveda accordingly).

As with the earlier portion of the Vedas, it is hard to determine exactly when these Upanishads originated. However, historians and theologians have looked at the flow of the language and have developed an order in which these Upanishads may have been developed. Chronologically, these Upanishads have been believed to have been developed as follows:.

- ♦ Brihadaranyaka Upanishad (Around 700 BC)

- ♦ Chandogya Upanishad (Around 600 BC)

- ♦ Taittiriya Upanishad (Around 500 BC)

- ♦ Aitareya Upanishad (Around 500 BC)

- ♦ Isha Upanishad (Around 400 BC)

- ♦ Kena Upanishad (Around 400 BC)

- ♦ Katha Upanishad (Around 400 BC)

- ♦ Prashna Upanishad (Around 200 BC)

- ♦ Mundaka Upanishad (Around 100 BC)

- ♦ Mandukya Upanishad (Around 100 BC)

Key Vedantic Glossary

Before we delve into the philosophical and spiritual teachings of each of these 10 Upanishads, we need to have a higher-level understanding of the key Vedantic concepts of Atman (Self) and Brahman (Ultimate Reality)

Atman (individual soul, self, or consciousness)

Who am I?

Atman is the profound *Upanishadic* answer to the most difficult question to answer. *"Who am I?"* Without realizing who you truly are, a spiritual journey to eternal bliss is not possible, per Vedantic teachings.

The concept of *"Atman"* (self or soul) is profoundly and uniquely covered in all the *Upanishads*. It is mind-boggling to imagine that the ancient Indian sages and scholars placed so much importance on the "inner self" rather than the "outer self," which includes the sensual experience that we are so used to in interacting with the world around us. This is placing the **subjective** experience above and beyond the **objective** experience to reach ultimate bliss or self-realization. This concept is considered one of the jewels of the *Upanishads*.

So, what exactly is this, *Atman*? Before we get into this life-changing concept, it is important to understand how Vedanta views the "you" or the "individual being."

The ***Taittiriya Upanishad*** *(Yajurveda)* describes that every individual being is made up of *Pancha Kosha* (5 sheaths or layers).

- Annamaya Kosha (physical sheath)

  Outermost sheath containing the physical body and the physical aspect of human existence.

- *Pranamaya Kosha* (Vital Life Force Sheath)

  Contains vital energy, breath, and life force.

- *Manomaya Kosha* (mental sheath)

  Contains mind, thoughts, emotions, ego, and intellect. Represents the mental aspect of human existence.

- *Vijnanamaya Kosha* (intellectual sheath)

  Contains discernment, intelligence, and wisdom. Represents the intellectual and discriminative aspects of human existence.

- *Anandamaya Kosha* (Bliss sheath)

  Innermost sheath, representing joy, bliss, and supreme happiness. Represents the blissful aspect of human existence and is closest to the true nature of the self (*Atman*).

  Underneath all these layers is thought to be the *Atman,* which is self-luminous.

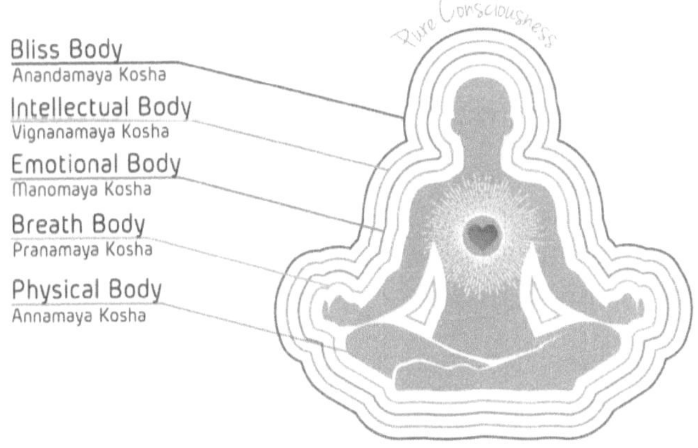

Various Upanishads also describe these five sheaths as different forms of matter or body. The "gross" body is made up of gross matter, the subtle body is made up of "subtle matter," and the causal body is made up of "causal matter."

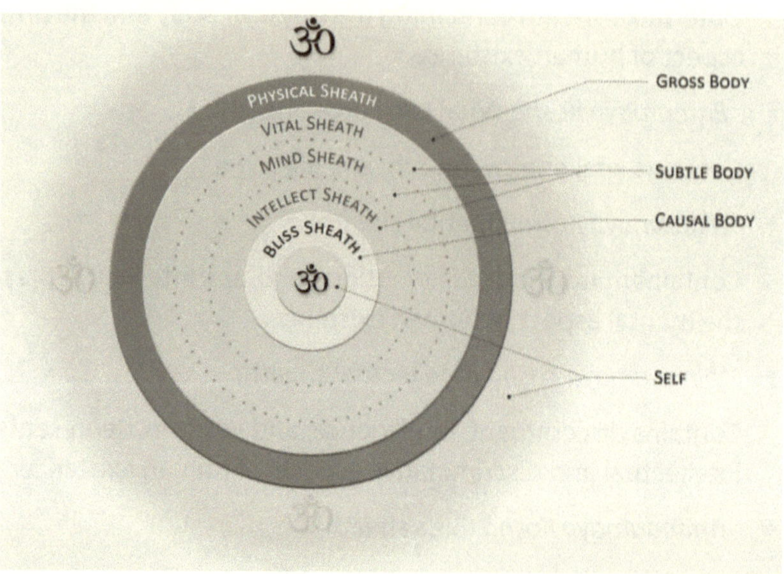

The gross body (*Sthula Sharira*) contains the physical aspect of our individual body.

The subtle body (*Sukshma Sharira*) is not visible to the senses. It consists of the life forces (Prana), mind, thoughts, intellect, and ego.

The causal body (*Karana sharira) is* the deepest and subtlest and is said to be the causal impact of an individual's existence. It is the repository of all past actions, deeds, and impressions (*karmas*).

Beyond all these sheaths is the self, or *Atman.*

According to various Upanishads, *Atman* is said to be

Infinite, imperishable, beyond the grasp of senses

(Brihadaranyaka, *Isha Upanishad, Katha Upanishad*)

Quote from Brihadaranyaka Upanishad

न वाचं न चक्षुषी नोत्तरं न तेजसि पाश्यति । तत्रैदानीं विषायान्वन्नाभ्युक्ता रेतः ॥

na vācaṁ na cakṣuṣī nottaraṁ na tejasi pāśyati | tatraidānīṁ viṣāyān vannābhyuktā retaḥ ||

"There the eye goes not, speech goes not, nor the mind. We know It not; we do not understand how It can be taught. It is different from the known; It is beyond the unknown.

Quote from Katha Upanishad

न जायते म्रियते वा विपश्चिन्नायं कुतश्चिन्न बभूव न भूयः ।

अजो नित्यः शाश्वतोऽयं पुराणो न हन्यते हन्यमाने शरीरे ॥

na jāyate mriyate vā vipaścinnāyaṁ kutaścinna babhūva na bhūyaḥ |

ajo nityaḥ śāśvato'yam purāṇo na hanyate hanyamāne śarīre ||

"The Atman is not born, and It does not die. It is not produced by anyone, nor does anyone come into existence from It. Unborn, eternal, everlasting, and ancient, It is not killed when the body is killed."

Eternal truth, the supreme goal of life, and realization lead to liberation (Moksha).

The concept of Atman is also covered in other major Upanishads with a relationship to *Brahman* (ultimate reality), which we will get to in the later sections.

Atman as being distinct from Body and Mind Stuff

Atman (self) is distinct from all the five sheaths described previously. This is a great revelation of the *Upanishads* that our pure self (*Atman*) is NOT the body or breath (Prana), or Mind (manas), or Thoughts (Chitta), or Intellect (Buddhi), or Ego (*Ahankara*).

The relationship between the Atman and the body and mind stuff is beautifully and poetically expressed in the *Katha Upanishad*. (1.3.3)

आत्मानँ रथितं विद्धि शरीरँ रथमेव तु ।

बुद्धिं तु सारथिं विद्धि मनः प्रग्रहमेव च ॥ ३ ॥

ātmānaṁ rathitam viddhi śarīraṁ rathameva tu |

buddhiṃ tu sārathiṃ viddhi manaḥ pragrahameva ca || 3 ||

"Know the *atman* as the lord of the chariot, the body as only the chariot, and intelligence as the driver; know the minds as the reins.".

Here it is implicitly assumed that the senses are the horses (sense of sight, smell, hear, touch, and speak) and the sense objects are the paths around them. If the horses (through sense control) are not restrained by using the reins (mind) through the driver (intelligence), the *Atman*, who is the lord of the chariot, guides the chariot (body) to the right path.

The *Katha Upanishad* then declares that "when the *Atman* (self) understands this and is integrated with body, senses, and mind, it becomes virtuous, mindful, and pure. This is the way to reach bliss, freedom, and liberation.

This mind control, or mind restraint, is very similar to the *Yoga Sutras* of Patanjali that were discussed as part of the *Yoga* school of Hinduism.

This relationship between *Atman* and the body-mind stuff is illustrated in the popular visual below:

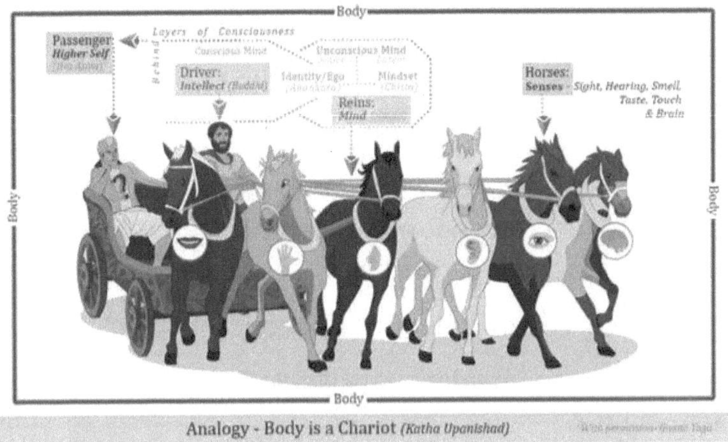

Analogy - Body is a Chariot *(Katha Upanishad)*

UPANISHADIC VIEW OF THE MIND

The Upanishads go deeper into breaking down the mind, or *Manomayakosha* (subtle matter), into deeper and subtler levels.

Manas (Mind, memory, Imagination)

Ahamkara (Ego or I-ness, or identity)

Citta (Thoughts, Emotions)

Buddhi (Intelligence)

A beautiful quote from the *Brihadaranyaka Upanishad* explains the *Atman* as follows:.

"You cannot see the seer of seeing;

you cannot hear the hearer of hearing;

you cannot think of the thinker of thinking;

you cannot know the knower of knowing.

This is yourself that is within all;

everything else but this is perishable."

This clearly states that our self (*Atman*) is beyond the comprehension of our body, mind, and intellect.

According to the Upanishads, the definition of the "self" or "I" or "individual being" is not the body, mind, ego, thoughts, or Buddhi but the *Atman*. We have learned from the famous verse above that only *Atman* is eternal, unchanging, and imperishable, and all the body and mind stuff changes and is perishable.

Our bodies constantly change and hence cannot be "I"

Our *Manas* (mind, memory, imagination) constantly changes and hence cannot be "I"

Our *Citta* (Thoughts) constantly change and cannot be "I"

Our *Buddhi* (Intelligence) constantly changes and cannot be "I"

Only Atman does not change, is eternal, and is the true "I".

This leads to the logical conclusion that for true realization of "I" or "self," one has to move beyond the notion of "I" we associate ourselves with.

"I am tall." "I am light or dark." "I am handsome." – Body

"I am successful." "I am rich." – Ahankara (Ego)

"I am happy." "I am sad." "I am angry." "I am jealous." – Emotions

According to Vedanta, none of the above are "I." Only the Atman is the true "I" or "self."

The above section answers the question, "Who am I really?"

However, more questions remain.

"If I am Atman, how do I realize it?"?

"Who is God, and how is God related to himself or Atman?"

Thankfully, the *Upanishads* have answers to these timeless questions, which we will dive deep into in the next chapter.

A simple visual depicting the mind, according to the *Upanishads*, is highlighted in the visual above.

BRAHMAN (GOD, ULTIMATE REALITY)

In the Vedas and Upanishads, Brahman is described as the ultimate reality in the universe, both immanent and transcendental. *Brahman* is defined as unchanging, pervasive, infinite, eternal truth, consciousness, and bliss.

Hundreds of hymns in the *Upanishads* describe Brahman extensively. No word or words can do justice to capture the essence of Brahman in the literary sense.

Brahman, as described by the Western Scholars

The famed writer Gavin Flood, summarizes the concept of *Brahman* in the Upanishads to be the "essence, the smallest particle of the cosmos and the infinite universe," the "essence of all things which cannot be seen, though they can be experienced," the "Self within each person, each being, the "truth," the "reality," the "absolute," and the "bliss."

Another famed Western philosopher, Paul Deussen, extends the meaning of Brahman to include metaphysical and cosmological aspects.

"Primordial reality that creates, maintains, and withdraws within it the universe"

"The ultimate is the cause of everything, including all gods."

"Essence and everything innate in all that exists inside, outside, and everywhere."

Brahman described in the Vedas

Perhaps the most significant verse highlighting one unchanging ultimate reality is in the Rig Veda (oldest of the Vedas)

एकं सद्विप्राः बहुधा वदन्ति। अग्निं यमं मातरिश्वानमाहुः।

ekam sad viprāh bahudhā vadanti,

agniṁ yamaṁ mātariśvānamāhuḥ,

"The wise speak of the One Reality in many ways; they call it Agni, Yama, Mātariśvan"

In this verse, the hymn acknowledges the diversity in the interpretation of the ultimate reality (the One) and the various manifestations or names attributed to it, highlighting a recognition of a fundamental unity amid diversity.

Chandogya Upanishad (3.141.) beautifully captures the universality of Brahman

सर्वं खल्विदं ब्रह्म

"All this is Brahman"

Brahman is beyond Space, Time & Causation

Upanishads describe Brahman as being devoid of any attributes (Nirguna Brahman)

Brahman, the supreme reality is infinite and hence is not bound by space, time or cause and effect.

This makes Brahman omnipresent, all-pervading and infinitely great.

These is summarized in these beautiful quotes from the *Kena Upanishad.*

Mantra 1.4

यद्वाचानभ्युदितं येन वागभ्युद्यते ।
तदेव ब्रह्म त्वं विद्धि नेदं यदिदमुपासते ॥ ४ ॥

yadvācānabhyuditaṃ yena vāgabhyudyate |

tadeva brahma tvaṃ viddhi nedaṃ yadidamupāsate || 4

"That which cannot be expressed by speech, but by which speech is expressed—That alone know as Brahman and not that which people here worship."

Mantra 1.5

यन्मनसा न मनुते येनाहुर्मनो मतम् ।
तदेव ब्रह्म त्वं विद्धि नेदं यदिदमुपासते ॥ ५ ॥

yanmanasā na manute yenāhurmano matam |

tadeva brahma tvaṃ viddhi nedaṃ yadidamupāsate || 5 *||*

"That which cannot be apprehended by the mind, but by which, they say, the mind is apprehended—That alone know as Brahman and not that which people here worship."

Mantra 1.6

यच्चक्षुषा न पश्यति येन चक्षूंषि पश्यति ।
तदेव ब्रह्म त्वं विद्धि नेदं यदिदमुपासते ॥ ६ ॥

yaccakṣuṣā na paśyati yena cakṣūṃṣi paśyati |
tadeva brahma tvaṃ viddhi nedaṃ yadidamupāsate || 6 ||

"That which cannot be perceived by the eye, but by which the eye is perceived—That alone know as Brahman and not that which people here worship."

Mantra 1.7

यच्छ्रोत्रेण न शृणोति येन श्रोत्रमिदं श्रुतम् ।
तदेव ब्रह्म त्वं विद्धि नेदं यदिदमुपासते ॥ ७ ॥

yacchrotreṇa na śṛṇoti yena śrotramidaṃ śrutam |
tadeva brahma tvaṃ viddhi nedaṃ yadidamupāsate || 7 ||

"That which cannot he heard by the ear, but by which the hearing is perceived—That alone know as Brahman and not that which people here worship."

Brahman is attribute-less and hence cannot be completely known by our mind alone

There is a profound but difficult verse from the *Kena Upanishad* (2.3)

"He by whom Brahman is not known, knows It;

he by whom It is known, knows It not.

It is not known by those who know It;

It is known by those who do not know It. (2.3) "

Spiritual master Yogananda writes a very powerful commentary on the above *Kena Upanishad* verse (2.3)

If a thing is endowed with a form or attributes, it can be expressed by words or comprehended by thought. But if it is devoid of these, all efforts of the mind and the sense organs to understand it are futile. Brahman is devoid of form, name, and qualities. Further, the mind itself is non-luminous: its apparent luminosity is derived from the light of Atman. Lastly, the power of the mind is limited. The more it contemplates Brahman and realizes Its true greatness and glories, the more it understands that it can never grasp Its full nature. To the illumined soul, therefore, Brahman remains, as it were, unknown. But the unillumined person, unable to comprehend Brahman, regards one of Its upadhis as Brahman and thus concludes that he has known Brahman. What he has known is in reality the mind, the buddhi, or some other upadhi of Brahman.

Another powerful verse from the Mundaka Upanishad emphasizes the attribute-less ness infinity that is *Brahman*.

यत्तदद्रेश्यमग्राह्यमगोत्रमवर्णमचक्षुःश्रोत्रं तदपाणिपादम् ।
नित्यं विभुं सर्वगतं सुसूक्ष्मं तदव्ययं यद्भूतयोनिं परिपश्यन्ति धीराः ॥ ६ ॥

yattadadreśyamagrāhyamagotramavarṇamacakṣuḥśrotraṃ
tadapāṇipādam |
nityaṃ vibhuṃ sarvagataṃ susūkṣmaṃ tadavyayaṃ yadbhūtayoniṃ
paripaśyanti dhīrāḥ || 6 ||

"That which cannot be perceived, which cannot be seized, which has no origin, which has no properties, which has neither ear nor eye, which has neither hands nor feet, which is eternal, diversely manifested, all-pervading, extremely subtle, and undecaying, which the intelligent cognized as the source of everything.

Brahman as the higher knowledge.

Brahman is referred to by Upanishads as "once known all things become known". There is a pivotal conversation in the *Mundaka Upanishad* between a spiritual seeker and the spiritual guru (Angiras)

कस्मिन्नु भगवो विज्ञाते सर्वमिदं विज्ञातं भवतीति ॥ ३ ॥

kasminnu bhagavo vijñāte sarvamidaṃ vijñātaṃ bhavatīti || 3 ||

"What is that my lord, by which being known, all of this becomes known?"

तस्मै स होवाच । द्वेविद्ये वेदितव्ये इति ह स्म यद्ब्रह्मविदो वदन्ति परा चैवापरा च ॥ ४ ॥

tasmai sa hovāca | dvevidye veditavye iti ha sma yadbrahmavido vadanti parā caivāparā ca || 4 ||

"Angiras told him, "Two types of knowledge a man should learn, those who know Brahman tell us — the higher (Para) and the lower (Apara)."

तत्रापरा ऋग्वेदो यजुर्वेदः सामवेदोऽथर्ववेदः शिक्षा कल्पो व्याकरणं निरुक्तं छन्दो ज्योतिषमिति ।अथ परा यया तदक्षरमधिगम्यते ॥ ५ ॥

tatrāparā ṛgvedo yajurvedaḥ sāmavedo'tharvavedaḥ śikṣā kalpo vyākaraṇaṃ niruktaṃ chando jyotiṣamiti |
atha parā yayā tadakṣaramadhigamyate || 5 ||

"Of these, the *Apara* (Lower knowledge) is the *Rig Veda,* the *Yajur Veda,* the *Sama Veda,* and the *Atharva Veda,* the *phonetics,* the code of rituals, grammar, *etymology, meter* and astrology. Then the *para* (higher knowledge) is that by which the immortal is known".

Higher knowledge is said to realize the immortal or Brahman. Note that this "Higher knowledge" is placed higher than just reading the Vedic scriptures.

So, what is this higher knowledge (para) that lets us know *Brahman?*

Now we come to the philosophical heart of the *Upanishads,* where the relationship between *Atman* and *Brahman* will be discussed as a way to realize the ultimate reality (*Brahman*)

BRAHMAN & ATMAN

Brahman is without form. How can Brahman be known? What is this higher knowledge (*para*) that lets us know Brahman?

Before we delve into the philosophical and spiritual teachings of each of these 10 Upanishads, we need to understand the different schools of Vedanta. The founders of these three schools of Vedanta looked at Upanishads from slightly different angles. Due to the extreme brevity and enormous meaning hidden behind every *shloka* (verse) of these *Upanishads,* these great scholars and philosophers wrote commentaries (*bhashyas*) on these to expand the meaning. While all these three *Vedanta* schools agree on the authority of the Vedas and Upanishads, there are some fundamental differences that need to be understood.

These three schools of thought differ in the relationship between two central themes in Vedanta:

- ◆ *Atman* (Self or Consciousness)

- ◆ *Brahman* (Ultimate Reality)

3 schools of Vedanta

Schools	Founder	Key Philosophy
Advaita (One without a second ,Monism)	Adi Shankaracharya (788-820 CE)	Atman & Brahman are the same
Vishishtadvaita (Qualified Monisim)	Ramanujacharya (1077-1157 CE)	Atman is part of Brahman but not identical
Dvaita (Dualistic)	Madhvacharya (1238-1317 CE)	Atman & Brahman are fundamentally different

Advaita Vedanta unequivocally declares that Brahman is the sole, unchanging reality and that there is no duality. Advaita means "one without a second" and is a very profound monistic philosophy founded by the great scholar and philosopher Adi Shankaracharya during the 8th century. It is the first *Vedanta* school of Hinduism.

Advaita Vedanta espouses that all of SELF, all of existence in space and time, is one and the same (one without a second). In essence, Advaita emphatically says that *Atman* (the inner self) and *Brahman* (the ultimate reality) are ONE AND THE SAME.

Brahman is the origin and end of all things, material and spiritual. *Brahman* is the root source of everything that exists. Advaita Vedanta states that *Brahman* can neither be taught nor perceived (as an object of intellectual knowledge), but it can be learned and realized by all human beings through *Jnana* (knowledge).

The goal of Advaita Vedanta is to realize that *Atman* (self) gets obscured by ignorance and false identification (*Avidya*). When *Avidya* is removed through *Jnana* (knowledge), the *Atman* is realized as identical to *Brahman*. Advaita Vedanta states that Brahman is within each person. *Brahman* is all that is eternal, unchanging, and that which truly exists.

Adi Shankaracharya propounded that:

"Universe does not magically get "created" by Brahman; universe *is* Brahman".

Shankaracharya taught that Brahman can be obtained through

♦ Knowledge of Brahman in the *Srutis (Upanishads)*

♦ Self-inquiry into the identity of "I"

The philosophical enormity of the Advaita Vedanta, along with the various Upanishadic descriptions supporting the Advaita philosophy, will be covered in the next chapter.

Adi Shankaracharya's philosophy of the unity of Atman and Brahman was very radical. Not everybody agreed with his point of view, and the first of the schools of thought in this non-monistic way of thinking was the *Visishtadvaita* philosophy founded by Sri Ramanujacharya in the early 12th century.

Visishtadvaita (qualified monism) believed in the monistic (Advaita) view that there is one Brahman (supreme reality), but offers a differing view that individual selves (Atman) are inherently different *but* part of *Brahman*. This philosophy can be summarized as 'diversity from one underlying unity."

Ramanujacharya asserts that the relationship between God and the individual self must be one of *Bhakti* (devotion), and *moksha* (liberation) is only attained by worship of Brahman (ultimate reality).

Brahman is also thought of as being of a personal nature who has attributes and can be worshipped (*Saguna Brahman* or *Ishvara)*.

Ramanujacharya stated,

"Those who surrender to the Supreme Person and are engaged in His devotional service, attain to that transcendental, eternal abode from which there is no return."

Unlike the Advaita Vedanta, which emphasizes *Jnana* (knowledge) for *Brahman* realization, the Visishtadvaita emphasizes *Bhakti* (devotion and worship) toward Brahman to achieve liberation.

The last major school of Vedanta is called *Dvaita* (Dualistic) and was propounded by renowned philosopher and theologian Sri Madhvacharya in the 13th century. Madhvacharya's Dvaita philosophy completely denies the monistic view of the Advaita Vedanta and emphasizes the clear distinction between the individual soul (referred to as *Jivatma)* and the supreme soul (*Brahman or Paramatma)*.

Dvaita Vedanta refers to *Jiva* as individual souls (*Jivatama*).

Each *Jiva* is distinct and eternal, separate from *Brahman*, and possesses its own unique characteristics, consciousness, and qualities.

Dvaita Vedanta presents the concept of *"Tattvavada"* (arguments from a realist viewpoint), which divides reality into three fundamental and distinct categories:

- God (Brahman),
- Individual souls (jivas)
- Matter (Jada)

These categories are ontologically and eternally separate.

Just like the *Visishtadvaita Vedanta*, *Brahman* is also thought of as being of a personal nature who has attributes and can be worshipped (*Saguna Brahman* or *Ishvara*).

Liberation (*Moksha*) in Dvaita Vedanta is achieved through devotion to the supreme Brahman and adherence to dharma (righteousness).

The philosophy of Dvaita Vedanta triggered a huge Bhakti movement in India. The Bhakti movement was a widespread socio-religious movement that emerged in medieval India, emphasizing love, devotion, and personal attachment to a chosen deity, often viewed as the Supreme Being.

In theological terms, Advaita Vedanta is termed "monistic," and Dvaita and Visishtadvaita are termed "monotheistic."

Monism believes in the oneness or universality of reality. Monism emphatically states that all apparently separate and diverse things, beings, or phenomena ultimately originate from, or are reducible to, a single and unified substance, essence, or reality. In the case of Advaita Vedanta, this is the universality of Brahman and Atman.

Mahayana Buddhism (one of the schools of Buddhism) also holds monistic views concerning the ultimate nature of reality. However, there is a big difference. Mahayana Buddhism emphasizes the oneness of all things and the interconnection of all beings, leading to emptiness

(Shunyata), radically different from the *Brahman* (ultimate reality) advocated by the *Advaita Vedanta.*

On the contrary, **monotheism** is the belief that there is only one deity, an all-supreme being that is universally referred to as God. The monotheistic God is considered supreme, omnipotent, all-knowing, and all-powerful. This deity is often seen as the source of all creation and the ultimate authority. In the case of Dvaita and Visishtadvaita Vedanta, this is "*Vishnu*" (*Saguna Brahman*, or *Brahman* with attributes, personal God).

Monotheism is the most popular religious system in the world. Major religions like Christianity, Judaism, and Islam are considered monotheistic.

The graphic below depicts the three major Vedanta schools with respect to the relationship between Atman and Brahman.

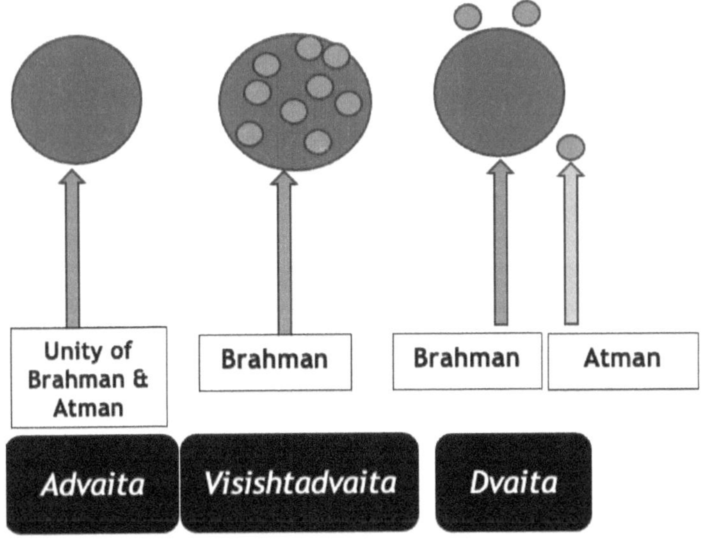

The Dvaita *Vedanta* propounded by Madhvacharya is radically different from both the *Advaita* and the *Visishtadvaita* philosophy. Dvaita claims that the individual soul (*Jivatma*) is different from the omnipotent Supreme Soul (*Paramatma*). Madhvacharya even claims that there are distinctions even among the *Jivas* themselves, and not every *Jiva* will achieve Moksha, or liberation. Another term for *Dvaita* is *TattvaVada* (realistic arguments). Madhvacharya propounds that only

Paramatma (the supreme soul) is independent (svatantra), and all the *Jivatma* (individual souls) are dependent (*asvatantra*) on the *Vishnu* (the supreme soul or God).

Madhvacharya postulates a personal God (Vishnu, Saguna Brahman). Moksha (liberation) in the Dvaita Vedanta is achieved through Bhakti Yoga, an intense devotion to the Supreme Lord, Vishnu.

Advaita Vedanta

This chapter offers detailed teachings of the Advaita Vedanta using the key Upanishads as the source.

This chapter also gives a high-level overview of some of the consequential work of Adi Shankaracharya.

The next part deals with a discussion of Neo Vedanta (modern Vedanta) that tries to find harmony with traditional Vedanta, western philosophy, and scientific exploration. Swami Vivekananda led the neo Vedanta movement in the late 19th century, which is the sole reason for the popularity of Vedanta in the Western world. Swami Vivekananda's teachings were deeply rooted in *Advaita Vedanta*, and he often stressed the universality of Vedantic principles.

Some of his great work and the tremendous impact of his work on the modern world will be discussed in the last section.

Upanishads as the source for Advaita Vedanta

Adi Shankaracharya propounded Advaita Vedanta in the early 8th century. That is almost 2000 years after the first Vedas were discovered.

Shankaracharya was one of the greatest saints and philosophers of India; he was the foremost exponent of Advaita ("non-dual") Vedanta, which proclaims the unity of the Atman (the Self) and *Nirguna Brahman* (the *Brahman* without attributes). His works elaborate on ideas found in the Upanishads. He was instrumental in the revival of Hinduism.

Advaita Vedanta draws on various Upanishads to prove the equality of Brahman and Atman. Of these, four main *mantras* (verses) are deemed

Mahavakyas (great sayings) and form the pillar of Advaita Vedanta philosophy.

Mahavakya #1 – Chandogya Upanishad part of the *Samaveda*

तत् त्वम् असि (Tat Tvam Asi)

"You Are That"

Mahavakya #2 – Brihadaranyaka Upanishad part of the *Yajurveda*

अहं ब्रह्मास्मि (Ahaṁ Brahmāsmi)

"I am Brahman."

Mahavakya #3 – *Aitareya Upanishad part of the Rigveda*

प्रज्ञानं ब्रह्म (Prajnanam Brahma)

"Brahman is Pragnana or Consciousness"

Mahavakya #4 – *Mandukya Upanishad part of the Atharvaveda*

अयम् आत्मा ब्रह्म (Ayam Atma Brahman)

"This self (Atman) itself is Brahman"

Advaita Vedanta has picked these 4 *Mahavakyas* from *Upanishads* in each of the four vedas to illustrate without a doubt the nonduality or unity of Self (Atman, Consciousness) and the Ultimate Reality (Brahman).

Mahavakya #1 – Tat Tvam Asi ("You Are That" or "That Thou Art")

The *Chandogya Upanishad* from the *Samaveda* makes a radical statement, which is one of the Mahavakyas. If we break this mantra down

Tat is "Existence" or "Brahman"

Tvam is "Self or "Atman"

Asi is "Are" "Identical"

Before we get into the details of the Chandogya Upanishad with this Mahavakya, it is important to understand the context of this Upanishad.

Svetaketu is the prime spiritual seeker in the *Chandogya Upanishad* and is the son of Uddalaka. The story goes that Svetaketu did not focus his mind on the study of the Vedas. His father sent him to the *Gurukula* (an *ashrama* whose purpose was to teach the *Vedas* to children at a young age). This is how the knowledge of the *Vedas* was passed on from one generation to the next.

Svetaketu went to the *Gurukula* at the age of twelve and studied the Vedas, scriptures, science, grammar, etc. at the feet of the Guru for twelve years, then returned home. He was very proud of his knowledge and scholarship, and he thought that he had finished studying everything. On seeing this attitude in his son, his father called him and thoughtfully asked a question: "O my son! Have you studied that thing knowing that everything becomes known?"

Svetaketu couldn't grasp this question clearly. He was eager to know *that,* by knowing that, everything else would become known. He also realized that he still had not learned the most essential things of the universe, and, with humility, he requested his father: "Father! May I request that you please teach me that most essential thing by which everything else becomes known?"

On hearing this reply from his son, the father (Uddalaka) slowly explained to him using simple examples: "Son! Have you not seen the clay in front of the potter's house? It becomes a pot in the hands of the potter. If the clay is known, then all things made of clay are known!

Similarly, if you know gold, things made of gold, like ornaments, are known. If you know iron, all things made of iron are known.

In the same way, if you know "Brahman," then all the things (the entire universe) that cannot exist without Him are also known." He continued his teaching and concluded with the statement, *Tat tvam asi.*

This mantra can be found in 6.8.7 of the Chandogya Upanishad as a conversation between the father Uddhalaka and his young son Svetaketu.

स य एषोऽणिमैतदात्म्यमिदं सर्वं तत्सत्यं

स आत्मा तत्त्वमसि श्वेतकेतो

sa ya eṣo'ṇimaitadātmyamidaṃ sarvaṃ tatsatyaṃ

sa ātmā **tattvamasi** śvetaketo

"That which is the subtle essence – in it all that exists has itself.

That is the Truth. That is the self. That Thou Art Svetaketu".

In this profound statement "That" (Tat) is said to contain the following attributes

- ♦ Subtlest or finest of all things
- ♦ Pure Existence
- ♦ Ultimate Reality
- ♦ Ultimate Truth

In very simple terms, the above terms are attributes of **Brahman.**

Tat represents *Brahman* (Ultimate reality) and

Tvam identifies the self (Atman).

Asi is an affirmation equating Brahman and Atman.

In very subtle terms, this *Mahavakya* tells us that by knowing the SELF (Self-realization) we will be able to recognize the entire universe because the universe cannot exist without the presence of Brahman.

Verse 6.9.2 further explains this *Mahavakya* in a beautiful example.

"Bees produce honey by collecting the juice from various flowers and mixing them together. Once the honey is formed, the identity of individual juice from individual flowers no longer exists.

When all beings attain unity in the self, they are not conscious of their diverse backgrounds. They attain unity in the Atman (Self)"

Verse 6.10.1 also explains this *Mahavakya* in another beautiful example.

"These rivers flow—the eastern toward the east and the western toward the west. They arise from the sea and flow into the sea. Just as these rivers, while they are in the sea, do not know: 'I am this river' or 'I am that river,'"Even so, all these creatures, even though they have come from Pure Being, do not know that they have come from Pure Being."

Unity of the Atman (self) - Unity in Diversity

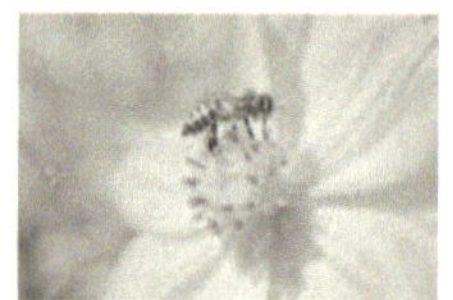

Chandogya Upanishad gives the above two beautiful examples to illustrate that all beings come from pure existence (Brahman) and are indistinguishable from the Brahman as only *Brahman* exists.

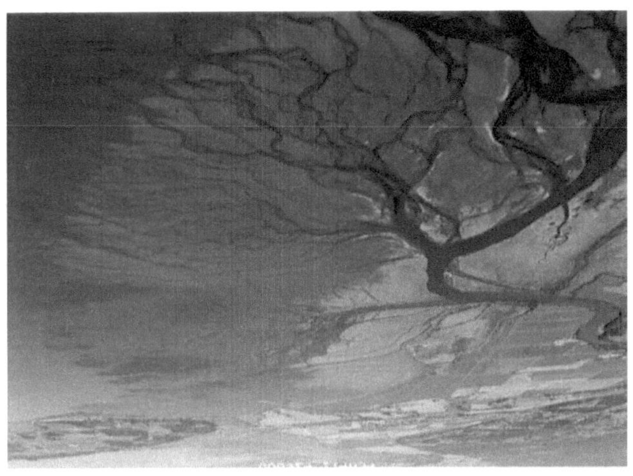

There is something common from which we have all come, on which we all rest, and into which we all go back. That something is always constant, which is the Brahman, or pure self, Atman.

The *Advaita* philosophy of Shankaracharya explains the plurality of the world as several names (Nama) and forms (Rupa) of the single indivisible entity.

This profound concept of *Maya* (superimposition) will be explained in a later chapter.

Mahavakya #2: Aham Brahmasmi (I am Brahman)

Arguably the most frequently used and most popular of the Advaita Vedanta philosophy is found in the above Mahavakya from the *Brihadaranyaka Upanishad* of the *Shukla Yajurveda*. Advaita Vedanta points to the above to illustrate the absolute oneness of *Atman* and *Brahman* in the same way a scientist or a mathematician puts forth proof to prove their theory or theorem.

The *Brihadaranyaka Upanishad* is revered for its depth of thought, intricate philosophical discussions, and guidance on spiritual realization, making it a significant scripture in the study of Vedanta and Indian philosophy. This Upanishad often presents philosophical teachings through conversations between sages and scholars. Notable conversations include those between the sage Yajnavalkya and his wife Maitreyi and between Yajnavalkya and other scholars. The above *Mahavakya* is revealed by the great sage Yajnavalkya in a conversation with his wife Maitreyi.

In the chapter on "Creation and Cause," Yajnavalkya mentions the following, which is profound and has deep philosophical meaning:.

A question is posed by Maitreyi:

"Men think, Through the knowledge of Brahman, we shall become all. Well, what did that Brahman know by which it became all?"

To this, Yajnavalkya responded:

ब्रह्म वा इदमग्र आसीत्, तदात्मानमेवावेत्, अहम् ब्रह्मास्मीति । तस्मात्तत्सर्वमभवत्; तद्यो यो देवानाम् प्रत्यबुभ्यत स एव तदभवत्, तथार्षीणाम्, तथा मनुष्याणाम्;

brahma vā idamagra āsīt, tadātmānamevāvet, **aham brahmāsmīti** |
tasmāttatsarvamabhavat; tadyo yo devānām pratyabubhyata sa eva
tadabhavat, tathārṣīṇām, tathā manuṣyāṇām;

"This [self] was indeed Brahman in the beginning. It knew itself only as "I am Brahman." Therefore, it became all. And whoever among the gods had this enlightenment, also became That [Brahman]. It is the same with the seers (rishis), the same with men. …And to this day, whoever in a like manner knows the self as "I am Brahman," becomes all this [universe]. Even the gods cannot prevent his becoming this, for he has become their Self."

Adi Shankaracharya unpacks this very complex philosophical statement that makes it easy to decipher.

"As in the world a form is revealed as soon as the observer's eye is in touch with light, similarly, the very moment that one has the Knowledge of the Supreme Self, ignorance regarding it must disappear. Hence, the effects of ignorance are impossible in the presence of the Knowledge of Brahman, like the effects of darkness in the presence of a lamp." Even Gods cannot stop the disappearance of ignorance on the attainment of Self-knowledge."

Mahavakya #3 – Prajnanam Brahma

(Brahman is Prajnana or Consciousness)

This Mahavakya is taken from the *Aitareya Upanishad* of the *Rigveda*.

Etymologically the Sanskrit word "Prajnana" can be divided into

"Pra" – "Higher" "Beyond" "Transcending"

"Jnana" – Knowledge", "Awareness", "Consciousness"

Prajnana can be interpreted as a higher or more profound level of knowledge, consciousness, or awareness, often implying a deeper or more transcendent understanding beyond ordinary knowledge.

According to the above Mahavakya, *Prajnana* (higher knowledge or consciousness) refers to the supreme and all-encompassing consciousness that is the essence of reality (*Brahman*).

Chapter 3 of the Aitareya Upanishad asks deep probing questions about the "Self"

"What is It that we worship as this Self? Which of the two is the Self?

Is It that by which one sees,

or that by which one hears,

or that by which one smells an odor,

or that by which one utters speech,

or that by which one tastes sweet or the sour?"

The Upanishad answers the question below:

"It (Self) is the heart and the mind. It is [known, in accordance with its different functions, as] consciousness, lordship, knowledge [of arts], wisdom, retentive power of mind, sense knowledge, steadfastness, thought, thoughtfulness, sorrow, memory, concepts, purpose, life, desire, longing [for sense objects]: all these are but various names of Consciousness (Prajnanam).

"This One is Brahman; this is Indra, this is Prajapati; this is all these gods; and this is these five elements, viz. earth, air, space, water, fire; and this is all these (big creatures), together with the small ones, that are the procreators of others and referable in pairs – to wit, those that are born of eggs, of wombs, of moisture of the earth, viz. horses, cattle, men, elephants, and all the creatures that there are which move or fly and those which do not move."

The *Mahavakya* is mentioned in the last verse below.

प्रज्ञानेत्रो लोकः प्रज्ञा प्रतिष्ठा प्रज्ञानं ब्रह्म

prajñānetro lokaḥ prajñā pratiṣṭhā prajñānaṃ brahma

All these have Consciousness as the giver of their reality; all these are impelled by Consciousness; the universe has Consciousness as its eye, and Consciousness is its end. **Consciousness is Brahman.**"

Philosopher David Loy sums up this Mahavakya beautifully.

"The *knowledge* of Brahman is not intuition of Brahman

but *itself* is *Brahman*."

Mahavakya #4 – Ayam Atma Brahma

(Atma is Brahman)

This Mahavakya is taken from the *Mandukya* Upanishad of the *Atharvaveda*.

Etymologically, this Mahavakya can be expanded as,

Ayam means "This"

Atman means "Self"

Brahman means "Ultimate reality."

This *Mahavakya* thus implies, "This self (Atman) is Brahman."

Mandukya Upanishad's importance to Advaita Vedanta

In a craftfully worded introduction to this Upanishad, Adi Shankaracharya (founder of the Advaita Vedanta) explains the purpose of this phenomenal Upanishad.

"As a man stricken with disease regains his normal health when the disease is removed, so Atman, identifying Itself with misery, recovers its normal state when the duality manifesting itself as the phenomenal universe is destroyed."

This realization of Non-duality (Advaita) is the end to be achieved. The manifoldness of duality is produced by avidya (Ignorance); it is destroyed by Vidya (the Knowledge of Brahman). Therefore, this treatise is begun for the purpose of revealing the Knowledge of Brahman.

The goal to be attained through the study of the Mandukya Upanishad is moksha or liberation. The means for its attainment is the practice of the knowledge of the identity of Brahman and Atman. This knowledge cannot be acquired directly through the study of scripture, yet scripture helps indirectly in this respect by demonstrating the unreality of the phenomenal universe and indicating the reality of Brahman. Thus, scripture, too, indirectly helps in the realization of Brahman.

Self-knowledge is eternally existent. But it appears to be non-existent on account of man's identification with the body, the mind, and other factors of the dualistic universe. This is all the result of avidya (ignorance). Under the influence of this false identification, a man regards himself as miserable and seeks happiness. Then, instructed by a compassionate preceptor, he practices the knowledge of non-duality (Advaita), which destroys the illusion of duality. When the obstructions created by duality are removed, he recovers Supreme Bliss, which is the very nature of Atman."

We will delve a bit deeper into the *Mandukya* Upanishad, as it is perhaps the most philosophical and deepest of the Upanishads. This Upanishad contains the most lucid definition of various states of consciousness and exactly who "I" or "self" is.

This Upanishad is also very unique as it starts with an analysis of the sacred syllable "AUM" (ॐ) (also spelled OM) and its connection with the various stages of consciousness.

This Upanishad is also the shortest of all the Upanishads, with only twelve verses, but is deemed to be supremely powerful. So, let's delve into it.

The first verse describes that *All is AUM.*

ॐ इत्येतदक्षरमिदँ सर्व तस्योपव्याख्यानं
om ityetad akṣaram idaṃ sarvaṃ tasyopavyākhyānaṃ

भूतं भवद् भविष्यदिति सर्वमोङ्कार एव ।
bhūtaṃ bhavad bhaviṣyad iti sarvam oṅkāra eva

यच्चान्यत् त्रिकालातीतं तदप्योङ्कार एव ॥१॥
yac cānyat trikālātītaṃ tad apy oṅkāra eva

"The whole universe is the syllable Om. Following is the exposition of Om. Everything that was, is, or will be is, in truth Om. All else which transcends time, space, and causation is also Om."

The word AUM consists of three syllables A, U and M.

A – Sound comes when you **Open** the mouth is the **beginning** sound

M – Sound comes when you **Close** the mouth and is the **final** sound

U – Sound comes as rolling **transition** of the mouth and is the **continuation** of sound

Therefore, when AUM is uttered, all various parts of the vocal organ are utilized, and it is said to include all sounds. Hence, the substratum of ALL words is AUM, and the substratum of the entire universe is *Brahman*.

It is said that the sounds signifying the phenomena (speech) are NO different from the phenomena itself (Brahman). It is, therefore, said that Brahman is AUM.

The second verse contains the Mahavakya.

सर्व ह्येतद् ब्रह्मायमात्मा ब्रह्म
sarvaṃ hyetad brahmāyam ātmā brahma

सोऽयमात्मा चतुष्पात् ॥२॥ 2..
so 'yam ātmā catuṣpāt

"All this is Brahman. **This Atman is Brahman.**

That which is this Atman has four parts"

The Mandukya Upanishad reveals that the Atman has four states. They are,

1. Waking State (*Jagruta*)

2. Dream State (*Swapna*)

3. Dreamless Sleep state (*Sushupti*)

4. State of Pure Consciousness (same as Brahman) (Turiya, or fourth state)

The four states are also associated with the syllables of AUM, as follows:

1. Waking State is associated with "A" (or the sound AAAAAAAAA).

2. The dream state is associated with "U" (or the sound UUUUUU).

3. Dreamless sleep is associated with "M" (or the sound MMMMMM).

4. The 4th state (Brahman or Atman) is associated with absolute silence that comes at the beginning or end of the syllable AUM.

It can be thought of as all sounds beginning in silence and ending in silence. That state of "soundlessness" is the Brahman, where all sounds originate and end. This profound concept is illustrated in this visual of the AUM.

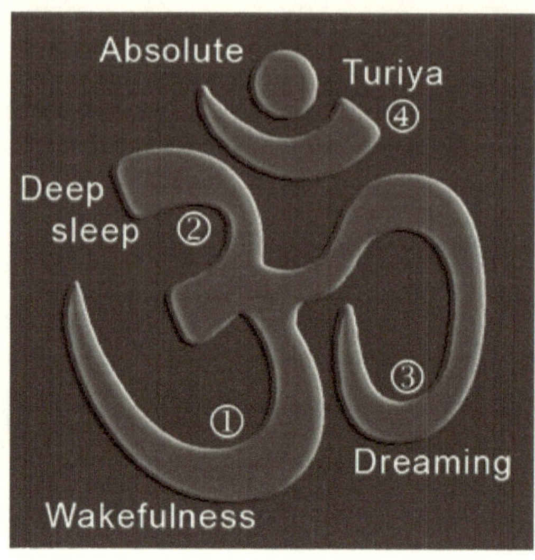

The third verse describes a very interesting concept of the attributes of the waking state of consciousness.

जागरितस्थानो बहिष्प्रज्ञः सप्ताङ्ग

jāgarita-sthāno bahiṣ-prajñaḥ saptāṅga

एकोनविंशतिमुखः स्थूलभुग्वैश्वानरः

ekona-viṃśati-mukhaḥ sthūla-bhug vaiśvānaraḥ

प्रथमः पादः ॥ ३ ॥

prathamaḥ pādaḥ

The first stage of Atman in the waking state is called Vaishvanara.

Vaishvanara can also be thought of as the "ego" or "identity" of Atman in the Waking state (Jagruta). In this state, consciousness is turned to the **external** world with seven limbs and nineteen mouths.

The seven limbs (described first in the Chandogya Upanishad) focus our consciousness externally in the waking state:

- ♦ Head – effulgent region
- ♦ Eyes – Sun
- ♦ Vital Breath – Air

- Middle Part of the body – space

- Kidney – water

- Feet – Earth

- Mouth – Fire

It can be noted that the seven limbs are a combination of the connection between the body and the universe as experienced by all of us in the waking state.

The nineteen mouths signify the instruments of *consumption*:

- 5 organs of perception, sense organs (eyes, ears, mouth, tongue, skin)

- – 5 organs of action – hands, feet, speech, reproduction, excretion

- 5 Vital forces (Prana) – Prana (inward breath), Apana (outward breath), Yana (circulation), Udana (Upward breath), and Samana (digestion)

- Mind (Manas)

- Intellect (Buddhi)

- Ego (Ahamkara)

- Thoughts (Citta)

To a casual reader, the idea of seven limbs and nineteen mouths sounds absurd, but only when you dig deep do you realize that Upanishadic knowledge is very subtle and profound. The above verse highlights all the attributes that comprise the waking state of consciousness.

स्वप्नस्थानोऽन्तः प्रज्ञः सप्ताङ्ग
svapna-sthāno 'ntaḥ-prajñaḥ saptāṅga

एकोनविंशतिमुखः प्रविविक्तभुक्तैजसो
ekona-viṃśati-mukhaḥ pravivikta-bhuk taijaso

The fourth verse describes the dreaming state of consciousness.

The second aspect of Atman (Consciousness) is the Self in the dreaming state (Svapna). The Self in this dreaming state is called *Taijasa*. In this state, consciousness is turned to a "subtler" "inner" world of dreams in the mental realm. Note that all seven instruments and nineteen channels are still engaged in the dream state.

At first, it might seem perplexing that in the dream state, our instruments of action and perception are still operational. Once you dig deep, you understand that the dreamer (*Taijasa*) has his own world of experiences. The dream appears perfectly real, as though in the waking state for the dreamer (*Taijasa*).

The dream state contains subconscious thoughts and desires. The Taijasa (Dreamer) experiences a realm of thoughts, emotions, and images, and the Taijasa state can present a diverse range of experiences and scenarios.

The fifth verse delves into the third aspect of the Atman.

सुषुप्तस्थान एकीभूतः प्रज्ञानघन
suṣupta-sthāna ekī-bhūtaḥ prajñāna-ghana

एवानन्दमयो ह्यानन्दभुक् चेतोमुखः
evānanda-mayo hyānanda-bhuk ceto-mukhaḥ

The third aspect of *Atman* is Self-operating in a deep sleep mode (*Sushupti*). The Self in this deep sleep state is called *Prajna*. In this state, there are no desires for any gross or subtle objects, and there are no dreams. All experiences have receded into undifferentiated consciousness. This state is filled with absolute bliss and can also lead to a clearer knowledge of the two preceding states.

The self, identified in the deep sleep condition, is called *Prajna*. *Prajna* seeks its joy not in the external sense objects as the waker, nor in the inner subtler objects like the dreamer. In this deep sleep condition, it enjoys a fullness of joy due to the complete absence of sorrow.

The Mandukya Upanishad describes this state of Prajna as a pure mass of bliss. There are no agitations of the external mind to cause sorrow or misery in the state. It is clear that the lack of outward sense objects that we identify with in the waking and the dream state is the primary reason for the pure bliss in the deep sleep state.

The sixth verse deals with the last state of the Atman or self.

एष सर्वेश्वर एष सर्वज्ञ एषोऽन्तर्याम्येष

eṣa sarveśvara eṣa sarvajña eṣo 'ntar-yāmyeṣa

योनिः सर्वस्य प्रभवाप्ययौ हि भूतानाम् ॥ ६ ॥

yoniḥ sarvasya prabhavāpyayau hi bhūtānām

"This is the Lord of all; this is the knower of all, this is the inner controller, this is the source of all. And this is that from which all things originate and in which they finally dissolve themselves."

The *This* from the previous verse is explained in the following 7th verse

नान्तःप्रज्ञं न बहिष्प्रज्ञं नोभयतःप्रज्ञ

nāntaḥ-prajñam na bahiṣ-prajñam nobhayataḥ-prajñam

न प्रज्ञानघनं न प्रज्ञं नाप्रज्ञम् ।

na prajñāna-ghanam na prajñam nāprajñam

अदृष्टमव्यवहार्यमग्राह्यमलक्षणं

adṛṣṭam avyavahāryam agrāhyam alakṣaṇam

अचिन्त्यमव्यपदेश्यमेकात्मप्रत्ययसारं

acintyam avyapadeśyam ekātma-pratyaya-sāram

प्रपञ्चोपशमं शान्तं शिवमद्वैतं

prapañcopaśamam śāntam śivam advaitam

चतुर्थं मन्यन्ते स आत्मा स विज्ञेयः ॥ ७ ॥

caturtham manyante sa ātmā sa vijñeyaḥ

"This is Not Conscious of the inner world,

Nor consciousness of the outer world

Nor conscious of both worlds

Nor dense consciousness, nor mere consciousness,

Nor unconsciousness"

"Unseen, non-relational, beyond grasp, indefinable, unimaginable, Indescribable, whose essence is every thought."

"In which worldly things are absent, silent, auspicious, non-dual- they consider it the fourth part. That is Atma. That is to be known."

There is never a more poetic and philosophical statement than in verse seven above, which truly describes what the fourth state (*Turiya*) is. The fourth state is the true self (Atman).

The great early 21st-century Neo Vedanta scholar and saint Swami Chinmayananda has summed this up beautifully.

"When the Conscious principle is projected out through the mind and intellect and through the sense organs, then it expresses itself in the Awareness of the world of objects and the world of ideas and thoughts. Remove this principle of awareness of Consciousness from a particular body; that body will no longer illuminate for itself the ideas of this outside world. This, we can say, not only in the scriptural language but as a scientific truth, that the world outside and world within rise up in this pure Consciousness, exist in this consciousness, and shall, when consciousness is withdrawn, merge back into Consciousness itself."

An example is illustrated on the next page. When consciousness (Atman) is projected through a prism of body, mind, and intellect, a plurality of the world appears. This is the waking and dream states explained in the previous verses.

The Advaita Vedanta philosophy of "why plurality" will be covered in a later chapter.

Consciousness - Unity to Diversity

Self Luminous

Body
Mind
Intellect

Plurality of
External World

The 8th verse to the 12th verse draw parallels to the syllable *AUM* and the four states of consciousness described in the previous seven verses.

सोऽयमात्माध्यक्षरमोङ्कारो
so 'yam ātmādhyakṣaram oṅkāro

ऽधिमात्रं पादा मात्रा मात्राश्च पादा
'dhimātraṃ pādā mātrā mātrāś ca pādā

अकार उकारो मकार इति ॥ ८ ॥
akāra ukāro makāra iti

"The same ATMAN is again AUM from the point of view of the syllables. The AUM with parts is viewed from the standpoint of its sounds or letters. The quarters are the letters, and the letters are the quarters. The letters here are A, U & M"

जागरितस्थानो वैश्वानरोऽकारः प्रथमा
jāgarita-sthāno vaiśvānaro 'kāraḥ prathamā

मात्राऽऽप्तेरादिमत्त्वाद् वाऽऽप्नोति ह वै
mātrā 'pter ādimattvād vā 'pnoti ha vai

सर्वान् कामानादिश्च भवति य एवं वेद ॥ ९ ॥
sarvān kāmān ādiś ca bhavati ya evaṃ veda

"He who is Vaisvanara having for his sphere of activity the waking stage is "A" the first letter of AUM, on account of its 'all pervasiveness' or on account of 'being the first' – these 2 are common features of both. One who knows this surely attains the fulfillment of all desires and becomes the first or the foremost among all."

The sound "A" is the most fundamental sound found in almost all languages. Even a newborn baby's first cry starts with 'A'. Thus, the word "A" is compared to the waking state as that's the "first" state once we are born in this world.

स्वप्नस्थानस्तैजस उकारो द्वितीया मात्रोत्कर्षाद्
svapna-sthānas taijasa ukāro dvitīyā mātrotkarṣād

उभयत्वाद्वोत्कर्षति ह वै ज्ञानसन्ततिं समानश्च
ubhayatvād votkarṣati ha vai jñāna-santatiṃ samānaś

भवति नास्याब्रह्मवित्कुले भवति य एवं वेद ॥१०
ca bhavati nāsyābrahmavit kule bhavati ya evaṃ veda

"He who is Taijasa, having for his sphere of activity in the dream state, is 'U' the second letter of AUM. On account of superiority or on account of 'being in between the two'. He who knows this attains to a superior knowledge and is treated equally by all and finds no one in his line of descendants who is not a knower of Brahman"

सुषुप्तस्थानः प्राज्ञो मकारस्तृतीया मात्रा
suṣupta-sthānaḥ prājño makāras tṛtīyā mātrā

मितेरपीतेर्वा मिनोति ह वा इदं सर्वमपीतिश्च
miter apīter vā minoti ha vā idaṃ sarvam apītiś ca

भवति य एवं वेद ॥११॥
bhavati ya evaṃ veda

"*Prajna*, whose sphere of activity is the deep sleep state is 'M', the third letter of AUM because it is the 'measure' and also 'that wherein all become one'. One who knows this identity of Prajna and 'M' is able to know the real nature of the things and beings, and also come to realize as being the Self of all"

And now the last verse (12) of the Mandukya Upanishad which discusses the 'fourth' state.

अमात्रश्चतुर्थोऽव्यवहार्यः प्रपञ्चोपशमः
amātraś caturtho 'vyavahāryaḥ prapañcopaśamaḥ

शिवोऽद्वैत एवमोङ्कार आत्मैव संविशत्यात्मना
śivo'dvaita evam oṅkāra ātmaiva saṃviśaty ātmanā

ऽऽत्मानं य एवं वेद ॥१२॥
'tmānaṃ ya evaṃ veda

"That which has no parts, the soundless, the cessation of all phenomena, all-blissful and non-dual AUM, is the fourth and verily it is the same as Atman. He who knows this merges his Self in the supreme Self, the individual in the total."

The partless, or AUM, is the soundless aspect and is the silence between successive AUMs. It is in this silence that all the sounds emerge, continue, and dissolve. This 'fourth' state is said to be eternal, immortal, and absolute bliss. The fourth state is characterized by the cessation of all phenomena associated with the body, mind, and intellect and is all-blissful due to the lack of external agitations and the plurality of the world.

Typically, the Advaita teachers also follow the Mandukya Upanishad with *Mandukya Karika,* which are the phenomenal works of Gaudapada, who was the teacher of Adi Shankaracharya's teacher (Govinda Bhagavatpada) and lived in the 600 CE.

Note that it was Gaudapada who coined the term 'Turiya" for the fourth state, as the Upanishad merely refers to it as the fourth state.

Gaudapada, in his "Mandukya Karika," extensively discusses the four states of consciousness: waking (Jagrat), dreaming (Svapna), deep sleep (Sushupti), and the transcendent state (Turiya). He emphasizes that the ultimate reality, Turiya, is beyond these states.

Gaudapada's teachings and writings had a profound influence on Adi Shankaracharya, the most prominent proponent of Advaita Vedanta.

Shankaracharya further developed and propagated the philosophy of Advaita Vedanta.

This book will not get into the details of the Mandukya Karika.

ADVAITA VEDANTA'S EXPLANATION FOR THE PLURALITY OF THE WORLD

Shankara (Adi Shankaracharya)
(788 – 820 CE)

We have extensively discussed the four Mahavakyas, and the Advaita Vedanta unequivocally declares that "Atman" and "Brahman" are the same. Adi Shankaracharya, the founder of the Advaita philosophy, propounds this truth in accordance with the authority of the Upanishads (*Sruti*) as well as one's own experience. The latter involves individual experiences of self-discovery, which Adi Shankaracharya proclaims will lead to the realization of unity of self with the *Brahman*.

In the Advaita Vedanta, self-realization and god-realization are used interchangeably as they mean the same thing.

How does the Advaita Vedanta explain the plurality of the world? This world is so full of plurality. This universe has so many attributes: living beings, animals, insentient things, nature, and the entire cosmos. How could there be a unity or a non-dual (one without a second) nature to this nature?

Adi Shankaracharya draws upon various of his works, including the works of his *Paramaguru* (Guru's Guru, Gaudapada), to make what is probably the most radical philosophy in the early 9th century to explain this non-duality or plurality.

- Only Brahman is real, while the plurality of the universe is *Maya* (illusion) due to the power of *Brahman.*

- The Power of *Maya* is a metaphysical principle and is like a veil that conceals the true, ever-luminous nature of the Atman (self).

- According to Shankaracharya, the power of *Maya* is *Anirvachaniya* (indescribable, inexplicable, and beyond conceptual understanding).

- Maya is the mechanism by which the ultimate reality, *Nirguna Brahman* (formless and attribute-less *Brahman),* 'appears' to take on many names (*Nama*) and attributes (*Rupa*), creating a plurality of the universe.

- The power of *Maya* leads to *Adhyasa* (superimposing the attributes and characteristics of the illusory world onto the ultimate reality, mistakenly perceiving the world as diverse).

- Not knowing the power of *Maya* hiding the true *Atman* is what Shankaracharya calls *"Avidya"* (ignorance), which leads to the illusion or falsity of the universe being viewed as plurality.

- Adi Shankaracharya propounds that *Moksha* (liberation, self-realization, and god-realization) can only be achieved by removing this ignorance (*Avidya*) through knowledge (*Jnana*).

One of the most famous examples given by Shankaracharya to describe Avidya in real life is of the 'snake and the rope' and is illustrated in the visual below.

During darkness, it is very easy to mistake a rope for a snake and be fearful. Only when there is light do you realize that it was rope all along?

Advaita Vedanta refers to the concept of *Adhyasa* (superimposition) to explain this phenomenon of mistakenly attributing characteristics or qualities of one thing to another.

Due to *Adhyasa* the darkness of *Avidya* Ignorance makes us think of our true selves as this illusory world of plurality (loaded with ups and downs) instead of the ever-blissful *Atman*that we truly are. Armed with the light of knowledge (Jnana), the illusory world is dispelled, revealing the true Brahman, or Atm.

Adi Shankaracharya writes,

"It is found in common experience that a rope, not known as such, is imagined in semi-darkness to be a snake, a line of water, a stick, or any one of a number of similar things. If the rope were previously known in its true nature, then the illusion of a snake or a stick would not have been possible. Similarly, *Atman* is imagined in various ways, for instance, as a *jiva* (living being) or as *prana* (life energy) , because of ignorance of Its true nature, the pure essence of Knowledge, which is non-dual and utterly unrelated to such phenomenal characteristics as causality etc., resulting in the experience of suffering and grief. This is the conclusion of *Vedanta*."

Another example that further illustrates the power of Maya.

This illustration further highlights that for a thirsty traveler in the desert, the mirage creates an illusion of water, just the same way the power of *Maya* due to *Avidya* (ignorance) drives living beings to seek the illusion of pleasures in the external world only to realize the emptiness of it.

Adhyasa (Superimposition) explained.

Adhyasa (superimposition or erroneous projection) is a pivotal concept in Advaita Vedanta. It helps explain how we perceive the world and ourselves in a way that is not aligned with ultimate reality (Brahman).

- *Maya* (a creative power or illusionary aspect of Brahman) causes *Avidya* (Ignorance)

- which leads to Adhyasa,

- mistakenly identifying self (Atman) with non-self (body, mind, and intellect) and

- the plurality of the universe rather than non-dual Atman or Brahman

This powerful concept is visualized in the following graphic.

Plurality of Universe - Explained

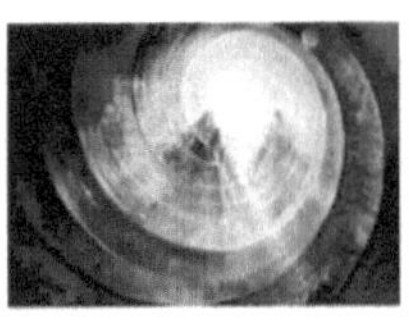

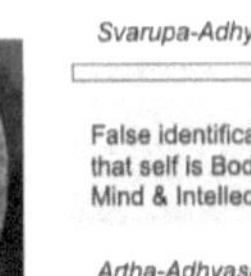

Nirguna Brahman (Form-less Attributeless Brahman)

Atman (True Self)

Veil covering the true nature of Atman

Maya (Creative or Illusory power of Brahman)

Another example of Adhyasa according to Advaita Vedanta is the analogy of Ocean and waves.

In this analogy, the 'ocean' represents the vast 'Brahman', which is the ultimate reality, infinite and un-divided. The waves that rise and fall in the ocean represent individual beings. Just as the waves temporarily appear and rise in the ocean to appear to be different from the ocean, individual beings (temporary) perceive they are different from the Brahman. This perception is due to avidya causing Adhyasa (superimposition), which falsely identifies waves as different from the ocean.

The wave erroneously identifies itself with its individual form, movement, and attributes, just as individuals (*jivas*) mistakenly identify themselves with their bodies, minds, and intellect. The wave forgets its essential nature as water, and in a similar way, individuals forget their essential nature as Brahman.

Eventually, the waves are nothing but the ocean, rise in the ocean, merge in the ocean, and are nothing apart from the ocean.

Similarly, Living beings (pure self, Atman) are nothing but Brahman; they rise in Brahman and merge in Brahman, and nothing is part of the Brahman.

The fundamental tenet of Advaita Vedanta is that, just as all waves are fundamentally made of the same water that constitutes the ocean, all individuals are essentially manifestations of Brahman. The distinction and separateness are merely apparent and not real. This illustrates the non-dualistic nature of reality in Advaita Vedanta.

Three levels of reality, according to Advaita Vedanta

One of the other profound philosophies of Shankaracharya explains the plurality of the world from the perspective of creation. This is termed the ontological criterion.

Shankaracharya proposes three levels of reality.

1. Absolute Reality (*Paramarthika*): *Brahman*

    Highest reality, which 'absorbs' all other reality levels. It is unchanging and infinite. This reality transcends time, space, and causality. In other words, this reality is timeless (ever-existent), spaceless (all-pervading), and not subject to cause and effect.

2. Pragmatic or relative reality (*Vyavaharika*):- *World*

    This reality is constantly changing over time and is the experience of all the worlds we live in. This is the reality where living beings (*Jiva*) and *Saguna Brahman* (personal God, or *Ishvara*) are present. This reality can be absorbed by absolute reality, indicating that this is a 'lower' level of reality.

3. Apparent or Unreality (*Prathibhashika*)

    This is the reality based on imagination alone, fabricated by the mind due to Adhyasa (superimposition). An example is falsely assuming a snake is a rope.

    John Grimes, a famous philosopher, explains the concept of Absolute and relative reality with a beautiful example of light and darkness.

From the perspective of the sun, there is no darkness; it is all light. It neither rises nor sets. From the perspective (relative) of the person on earth, there is a clear sunrise and sunset followed by light and darkness, respectively. Both realities are right from their perspectives but are contradictory. According to Advaita Vedanta, this does not mean that there are two versions of the truth; it only means that the same reality can be experienced from two different (relative) perspectives.

Similarly, from *Brahman's* perspective (absolute reality), the world is non-dual. There is nothing outside of *Brahman*. But from the perspective of living beings (*Jiva's*), there is plurality. Only when the *Jiva* realizes the true nature of self as Atman and equality with Brahman will the absolute and highest non-dual reality be reached.

Adi Shankaracharya wrote prolifically and composed many commentaries on the ten Mukhya Upanishads, the *Bhagavad Gita*, and the *Brahmasutras*, highlighting the non-dual nature of Brahman. He also wrote *Prakarana Granthas* (his own dissertations) to convey specific philosophical concepts in a more systematic and organized manner. Some key teachings coming from his *Prakarana Grant* wholeheartedly support his notion of the Advaita Vedanta.

It is justifiably hard to condense the profound teachings of Adi Shankaracharya into a few quotes. Some of his priceless teachings come in the various commentaries on the Upanishads and the *Prakarana*

Granthas. However, the following verses try to select a few golden verses from his *Prakarana Granthas.* The curious reader can refer to the vast references to Adi Shankaracharya's work in the references section at the end of this book.

Nirvana Shatakam (Atma Shatakam):

The Nirvana Shatakam, also known as the Atma Shatakam, is a profound composition in which Shankaracharya negates various aspects of the self, ultimately declaring the true nature of the self (Atman).

"Mano Buddhi Ahankara Chitta Ninaham, Nacha Shrotra Jihve Na Cha Ghrana Netre..."

"I am not the mind, intellect, ego, or memory, I am not the ears, tongue, nose, or eyes..."

DAKSHINAMURTI STOTRAM:

The Dakshinamurti Stotram praises Lord Dakshinamurti, the silent teacher and embodiment of knowledge.

"Vishvam Darpana Drishya Maana Nagari Tulyam Nija Antargatam..."

"The entire universe is reflected within the mirror of the Self, which is within me."

Aparokshanubhuti:

Aparokshanubhuti is a profound treatise on self-realization, elucidating the steps to attain direct perception of the self (Atman).

"Brahma Satyam Jagan Mithya Jivo Brahmaiva Na Aparah..."

"Brahman (the ultimate reality) is real, the world is an illusion, the individual self (Jiva) is nothing but Brahman."

VIVEKACHUDAMANI:

Vivekachudamani is a philosophical text that addresses the importance of discrimination between the real and the unreal.

"Jantunam Narajanma Durlabham Atma Satsadhakam..."

"Human birth is rare, and even rarer is the desire for liberation, and rarer still is the willingness to strive for one's own realization."

Liberation (Moksha)

The spiritual seeker might want to know, once reading all these scriptures, a concise summary or steps that need to be followed to reach eternal bliss, or Self-realization or God-realization.

An astute seeker might go one step further and wonder *what* the real *purpose* of these teachings of Vedanta, or Advaita Vedanta, is, to be specific.

The first question is the WHAT and HOW, and more importantly, the second question is WHY.

In this section, we will cover the WHY by explaining the Vedantic term *Moksha* (Liberation)

The etymological definition of *Moksha* is Freedom or Liberation. Freedom from what one might ask?

According to the Upanishads, it is freedom from the cycle of births and rebirths (referred to as *samsara*) and the 'enlightenment' that this freedom brings. Moksha is also freedom or liberation from ignorance and is the state of eternal bliss that transcends the body, mind, and intellect and is the unity of the self with the *Brahman* (ultimate reality).

The Upanishads don't specifically use the term *Moksha* but instead use synonyms' like

Mukti: Liberation

Amrita: Immortality

Nirvana: Bliss

Kaivalya: Oneness with the Absolute

The repeated cycle of births and rebirths does not seem like just an ominous thing to be liberated from. However, Vedanta claims that the living world is inherently characterized by suffering, dissatisfaction, and impermanence. People experience various forms of suffering—physical, mental, and emotional—due to desires, attachments, and the transitory nature of worldly experiences. It's the liberation from this material world to the non-transient blissful state or union with Brahman that Vedanta terms Moksha. Individuals are seen as bound by desires, attachments, egos, and ignorance. *Moksha* is liberation from these bonds, allowing one to live in harmony with the true nature of reality and attain a state of ultimate freedom and fulfillment.

The Upanishads proclaim loudly that Atman, or true self, never dies. The repeated births and rebirths (termed as *samsara*) are only for the body and the mind. Atman never dies, but according to Vedanta, he transmigrates to another body and mind due to the law of karma. This cycle continues perpetually until *Moksha* (liberation) is attained. The fundamental goal of a living being, according to Vedanta, is to try to achieve Moksha, the steps for which will be discussed in the next chapter (from an *Advaita* perspective).

Karma is a colloquial term in modern English and means 'cause and effect'. *Karma* only means that any actions we are involved with, whether they be physical, mental, or spiritual (cause), will have an imprint (effect) on our present or future lives. The imprint that our actions leave will continue perpetually till the human soul achieves *Moksha* (liberation). This concept of *Karma* is one of the fundamental tenets of Hindu philosophy.

HOW TO ATTAIN MOKSHA (LIBERATION) ACCORDING TO ADVAITA VEDANTA

The previous section discussed the answer provided by Vedanta to a burning question in any spiritual seeker's mind.

'Why' does every living being strive to attain *Moksha*?

Now armed with a convincing answer and the authority of the *Upanishads*, Shankaracharya discusses the HOW to get there.

In his famed *Prakarana Grantha* called Vivekachudamani (Crest Jewel of Discrimination), Shankaracharya lists four essential disciplines for a spiritual seeker on the path of Moksha.

1. Viveka (Discrimination): Discern between transient and eternal; unreal and the real

2. Vairagya (Detachment): Detachment from the material world and desires

3. Shad Sampat (6 virtues)

   1. Samah (calmness of mind)

   2. Damah (self-restraint and regulating behavior to align with ethical and moral principles)

   3. Uparati (withdrawal of mind from external distractions)

   4. Titiksha (Endurance. Accepting and enduring difficulties with equanimity and inner strength.)

   5. Shraddha (faith): faith in the scriptures and the Guru (teacher)

   6. Samadhana (concentration): meditation

4. Mumukshatva (Desire for Liberation)

According to Shankaracharya, once the spiritual seeker is armed with these 4 essential disciplines, Moksha can only be obtained by removing ignorance (Avidya) from knowledge (Jnana).

True knowledge is a direct, permanent realization that the Atman and Brahman are one. This realization instantly removes ignorance, leads to *moksha*, and is considered timeless, eliminating the cycle of birth and death (*samsara*). Advaita Vedanta emphasizes *Jnana Yoga* as the means of achieving *moksha*.

Jnana Yoga (yoga of knowledge and wisdom)

Jnana Yoga, according to Advaita Vedanta, is one of the main spiritual paths that emphasize knowledge, wisdom, and understanding as the means to attain liberation (*Moksha*). This path is considered the most direct path to realizing one's true nature and the oneness of the individual soul (*Atman*) with the ultimate reality (*Brahman*).

Advaita Vedanta focuses more on the direct experience of the individual (*Anubhava*) to discern the real and unreal to attain *Moksha*. It places more emphasis on self-inquiry (*Vichara*) than 'blind belief' in God's realization.

Shankaracharya and the Advaita Vedanta emphasize that the *Jnanayoga* consists of three main practices:

1. *Sravana* (Hearing and Absorption)

2. *Manana* (contemplation and deep reflection)

3. *Nididhyasana* (meditation and self-inquiry)

This three-step methodology is rooted in the teachings of Chapter 4 of the *Brihadaranyaka Upanishad* and draws great parallels to even the most scientific studies of modern times.

- ◆ *Sravana* refers to hearing, perception, and observations from a teacher (Guru) and involves discussing ideas and concepts.

- ◆ *Manana* refers to thinking about these discussions and contemplating the various ideas based on them, and is typically focused on self-study (svadhyaya).

- ◆ *Nididhyāsana* refers to meditation, realization and consequent conviction of the truths, non-duality, and a state of perfect unity with Brahman.

Jnana Yoga in Advaita Vedanta is a rigorous personal, intellectual, and experiential pursuit aimed at direct realization of the ultimate reality, leading to liberation and the cessation of the cycle of birth and death (samsara). It emphasizes knowledge (*Jnana*) as the key to self-realization and the path to experiencing the profound unity of the self (*Atman*) with *Brahman*.

What does attaining *Moksha* or *Brahman* mean?

Advaita Vedanta proclaims that the ultimate reality (Brahman) is Nirguna (without attributes). We have discussed the various attributes, or lack thereof, described in the various Upanishads in the previous chapters.

Brahman cannot be described but can only be experienced. What does that experience feel like? Advaita Vedanta explains three key aspects of Brahman.

1. **Existence *(Sat)* सत्:**

   Sat refers to "existence" or "being." And signifies the essential, absolute, non-dual eternal reality that transcends time, space, and causation. It is the ultimate and unchanging existence.

2. **Consciousness *(Chit)* चित्:**

   Chit translates to "consciousness" or "awareness." It represents the self-aware and self-luminous nature of Brahman. Brahman is not only existence but is also conscious and aware. It is the substratum of all intelligence, perception, and consciousness.

3. **Pure Bliss *(Ananda)* आनन्द:**

   Ananda means "bliss" or "joy." It signifies the intrinsic, eternal, and boundless happiness or bliss that is inherent in Brahman. This bliss is beyond pleasure and pain; it is a state of pure happiness.

In summary, "Sat-Chit-Ananda" encapsulates the understanding that the ultimate reality, Brahman, is eternal existence (Sat), self-aware consciousness (Chit), and boundless bliss (Ananda).

This emphasizes the indivisible, transcendent, and supreme nature of Brahman, beyond all dualities and limitations. These three states are the true goal of Moksha (*liberation*).

Karma Yoga and Bhakti Yoga

We have primarily discussed *Jnana Yoga* as the direct path to Moksha (liberation) according to Advaita Vedanta. The Upanishads and *Bhagavad Gita* (which contain Upanishad teachings from the personal god *Krishna*) also discuss two other paths for liberation. Karma Yoga and Bhakti Yoga

The Upanishads only provide an implicit definition of Karma Yoga and Bhakti Yoga; the more detailed and systematic elaborations are only found in later texts like the *Bhagavad Gita*.

Karma Yoga (Yoga of Action)

Karma Yoga is the path of selfless action and service performed without attachment to the outcomes of the actions. It is about dedicating one's actions to the divine or to the greater good of humanity.

Karma Yoga involves:

♦ *Selfless Action:* Performing actions without selfish motives, desires, or expectations of personal gain.

♦ *Duty (Dharma):* Adhering to one's duties and responsibilities as per one's role in society and the cosmic order.

♦ *Detachment:* Practicing detachment from the results of actions, focusing on performing one's duty diligently.

The goal of Karma Yoga is to purify the mind, develop selflessness, and attain spiritual growth while engaged in worldly duties. The *Bhagavad Gita* discusses Karma Yoga in greater depth, and one of the most famous verses from Chapter 2 of the Bhagavad Gita talks about Karma Yoga.

"कर्मण्येवाधिकारस्ते मा फलेषु कदाचन |

मा कर्मफलहेतुर्भूर्मा ते संगोऽस्त्वकर्मणि ||"

"Karmaṇy-evādhikāras te mā phaleṣhu kadāchana

Mā karma-phala-hetur bhūr mā te saṅgo 'stvakarmaṇi"

"Your right is to perform your duty only, but never to its fruits.

Let not the fruits of action be your motive, nor let your attachment be to inaction."

Bhakti Yoga: (Yoga of Devotion)

Bhakti Yoga is the path of devotion, deep, heartfelt love, and surrender to a chosen deity or the divine. It involves cultivating a personal, loving relationship with the divine. It usually involves a personal GOD (*Isvara* or *Saguna Brahman*, *Brahman* with attributes and form).

Bhakti Yoga typically involves:

♦ *Devotion:* Wholehearted devotion, love, and surrender to a personal god or the divine in any form or attribute.

♦ *Prayer and Rituals:* Engaging in prayers, rituals, singing hymns, and other devotional acts to express love and reverence for the divine.

♦ *Faith and Trust:* Having unwavering faith and trust in the chosen deity as a source of love, protection, and guidance.

The goal of Bhakti Yoga is to develop selflessness and attain union with the divine through a loving relationship, surrender, and intense devotion, often leading to self-realization and liberation.

Advaita Vedanta views on Karma Yoga:

Shankaracharya and the Advaita Vedanta emphasizes *Jnana Yoga* as a "higher" and more direct path to self-realization than *Bhakti Yoga* and *Karma Yoga,* while not entirely dismissing these two paths.

Shankaracharya viewed *Karma Yoga* primarily as a preparatory step for the higher path of Jnana Yoga. Engaging in selfless actions helps purify the mind and reduce desires, making it easier for individuals to turn inward and contemplate the nature of reality. Shankaracharya emphasized that the ultimate reality of Brahman is beyond time, space, and causation (Karma), and hence the seeker must transcend both action and inaction to realize the non-dual truth through *Jnana Yoga.*

Shankaracharya acknowledged that the earlier portion of the Vedas that was more action-oriented (Karma Kanda) was useful as part of the 4-fold "preparatory "steps (discussed in the previous section) to prepare the mind for the ultimate path, which is Jnana Yoga.

He emphasized that, at the appropriate stage in one's life, when the key mental qualities have been attained (using the preparatory steps) and one has fulfilled the duties (*Dharma*) of a householder, husband, father, etc., then actions (*karma*) serve no further useful purpose.

He strongly argued that action (that involves the self) and knowledge (selflessness) are contradictory.

Action necessarily causes one to identify with the body, even if this is subconscious. In the *upadesha sahasri (one of Shankara's Prakarana grantha)*, Shankaracharya says that action (Karma), in turn, brings about pleasure and pain as the results of the action. If the result is pleasurable, a desire to repeat the action is born; if it is painful, aversion results. Thus, further actions are generated, and the cycle goes on.

This cycle of karma accumulates, and further rebirth is needed, causing the cycle of *Samsara (repeated births)*. Action (karma) alone can never lead to *moksha*. Desires and aversions cannot be removed until avidya (ignorance) has been destroyed. This avidya (ignorance) conceals the fact that the self is an unlimited *Brahman,* which causes living beings to search endlessly trying to find happiness in transient, material things.

If one thinks that I am a 'doer' and an enjoyer, there is still ignorance. Therefore, *Jnana* is, in a sense, the opposite of *karma* because it entails the realization that I do nothing. The *Jnani* (seeker practicing *Jnana Yoga*) continues to perform his worldly duties and outwardly appears to act in the same way as before, but he knows that he is not the doer and therefore incurs no *karma*. Anyone who regards *karma* as a means to the end of realization necessarily still thinks of himself as a doer and therefore *prevents* realization.

Shankaracharya points out that action (*karma*) must involve ego (sense of I). A doer has a desire or aversion and chooses to act, and the action (karma) depends upon the doer. Knowledge, he argues, is quite different; no choice is involved. Knowledge depends on the object itself.

Knowledge brings with it the understanding that I am not a doer, and the Jnana *Yoga always* involves renouncing action as it transcends time, space, and causality (which is the action of cause and effect).

ADVAITA VEDANTA VIEWS ON THE BHAKTI YOGA

Shankaracharya and the Advaita Vedanta also saw *Bhakti Yoga* as a preparatory step for the higher practice of Jnana Yoga. Genuine devotion (*Bhakti*) to a personal deity or an impersonal form of the divine can help purify the mind and develop concentration, making it easier to engage in Jnana Yoga (self-inquiry and contemplation). His teachings encouraged individuals to choose an *Ishta Devata* (personal deity) of their liking and engage in heartfelt devotion toward that form. By dedicating their actions, thoughts, and emotions to the chosen deity, seekers cultivate a sense of surrender and attachment to the divine.

Shankaracharya acknowledged the efficacy of *Bhakti Yoga* in purifying the mind and instilling devotion but emphasized that the path to ultimate liberation is beyond devotion and non-devotion and is only possible through Jnana Yoga.

Bhakti Yoga is the most popular principle for all monotheistic religions, including the Dvaita Vedanta.

In summary, three paths to realization of the ultimate reality (Brahman): Jnana Yoga, Bhakti Yoga, and Karma Yoga all involve

- Losing the sense of I, selflessness
- Transcending beyond the body, mind, and intellect
- Transcending time, space, and causality.

The only thing that remains in the state is the true self, which is the ultimate Brahman. This is illustrated in the next visual.

The light here represents the true self (Atman).

The wax represents the I-ness (false association with the material world).

The goal is to use Jnana (knowledge), Karma (selfless actions), and Bhakti (devotion and surrender to personal God) to melt the I-ness so the only thing that remains is your true self.

SUMMARY OF ADVAITA VEDANTA AND SHANKARACHARYA'S TEACHINGS

This is best summarized in this visual.

The Advaita *Vedanta* views devotion (Bhakti) and selfless action (Karma) as preparatory steps that purify one's heart and mind. Jnana Yoga through self-inquiry and deep meditation is vigorous and needs equanimity of the mind to make progress.

How to attain Liberation according to Advaita Vedanta

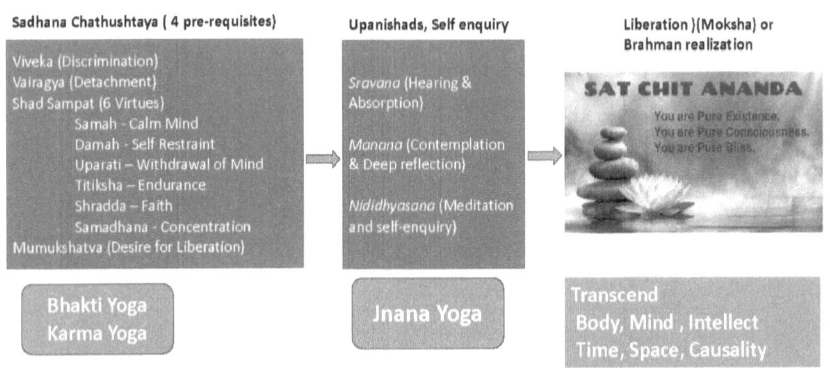

Chapter 5

BHAGAVAD GITA

INTRODUCTION

"The *Gita* is a like a bouquet composed of beautiful flowers of spiritual truths collected from the *Upanishads*"

– Swami Vivekananda

The *Bhagavad Gita* (Song by God) is one of the holiest and most profound scriptures in the history of religion. Just like the Vedas and Upanishads, it is hard to pinpoint the exact date of origin of the Bhagavad Gita. There is little doubt among scholars that the Gita was composed after the Upanishads, as the Gita reiterates some of the Upanishadic teachings. Adi Shankaracharya propounds the relationship between the Bhagavad Gita and Upanishads beautifully, in a very poetic fashion.

"sarvopaniṣado gāvo dogdhā gopālanandanaḥ
pārtho vatsaḥ sudhīrbhoktā dugdhaṃ gītāmṛtaṃ mahat"

"All the *Upanishads* are the cows; the son of the cowherd, namely Krishna, is the milkman; Partha (another name for Arjuna) is the calf; and the wise are the drinkers of the milk of the *Gita*, which is like nectar."

Historians concur that there is definitely a historical context to the Bhagavad Gita, and the consensus is that the composition might have happened a few hundred years BCE.

Famed English philosopher Aldous Huxley, like many other Western philosophers, proclaims that the *Bhagavad Gita* is the most systematic scriptural statement in the history of the world. The *Bhagavad Gita*, also called the *Gita*, is one of the principal scriptures in the *Vedanta* philosophy and forms the *Prasthana Trayi (the* Triple Canon of *Vedanta)* along with the *Upanishads and the Brahmasutras.* No topic in *Vedanta* is complete without the study of the *Gita.* We covered *Upanishads* in the previous chapter, and we will delve into the essential teachings of the *Bhagavat Gita* in this chapter. This book will not discuss the *Brahmasutras* owing to their complexity and the advanced nature involved in such a study.

We discussed extensively the importance of the *Vedas* and *Upanishads* as part of the Hindu school of religion. They are called *Sruti,* referring to "that which is heard" over perennial generations from master to student and eventually tracing back to God himself. *The Vedas* and *Upanishads* are also termed *Sruti Prasthana* and are the most sacred and divine teachings of Hindu philosophy.

The Gita, on the other hand, is classified as belonging to history (*itihasa*) and is part of the most epic poem ever written, the Mahabharata. The Mahabharata is a historical epic containing over 100,000 slokas, or 200,000 verse lines. The stories of the Mahabharata are folklore in the Hindu tradition, and the historical characters (both good and bad) are etched in the memory of the young and old in the Hindu religion. The Mahabharata and Ramayana (another preceding historical work) have profoundly shaped the culture of Hindu tradition and religion.

The Mahabharata features Lord Krishna, and the Ramayana features Lord Rama as one of the incarnations of the supreme Lord and revered deities in the Hindu religion. The Bhagavat Gita is part of the Mahabharata epic and stands tall as the cream of the philosophical teachings. The Bhagavad Gita portrays the philosophical teachings given by Lord Krishna (God incarnation) to Arjuna (the warrior prince and brother of the righteous *Pandava* brothers) on a battlefield. There are no other religious and philosophical teachings that have been given in the midst of a battlefield, signifying not the violent nature but the battles of everyday life that all of us deal with.

The Bhagavad Gita is the most practical advice given by the Godhead *Krishna* to *Arjuna*, and the uniqueness of the *Gita* is that Lord Krishna is actually speaking to every one of us through Arjuna. Arjuna's questions, albeit on a battlefield, are the questions of humanity, ones that most of us have. That's what makes the *Gita* the most timeless and practical scripture. As Mahatma Gandhi (father of the Indian Nation) said, "When doubts haunt me, when disappointments stare me in the face, and I see not one ray of hope on the horizon, I turn to *Bhagavad Gita* and find a verse to comfort me, and I immediately begin to smile in the midst of overwhelming sorrow. Those who meditate on the Gita will derive fresh joy and new meanings from it every day."

Akin to the many schools of Hinduism, there are many interpretations of the *Bhagavad Gita* from both a dualist (*Dvaita*) and monistic (*Advaita*) perspective, where Lord Sri Krishna is revered as the supreme reality in the former and as a Saguna Brahman (a symbolic representation of personal God) but not compromising on the oneness of the Brahman (ultimate reality) and the Self in the latter. The *Bhagavad Gita* is very terse (700 verses spread across eighteen chapters) and hence is open to interpretations, and the immersive spiritual seeker can find verses in the *Gita* that corroborate both of these versions unapologetically. We will not, however, delve into these differences but rather focus more on the philosophical teachings from Lord Sri Krishna that have been reinforced in the *Upanishads*.

Philosophers and theologians have structured the eighteen chapters of the Bhagavad Gita into the three major paths of yoga that have been discussed in the earlier chapters.

Karma Yoga & Dhyana Yoga– Chapters 1 through 6

Yoga of selfless action, Yoga of meditation

Bhakti Yoga – Chapters 7 through 12

Yoga of Devotion to the supreme reality

Jnana Yoga – Chapters 13 through 18

Yoga of knowledge

There is no uniform consensus in this classification, as some of the chapters cover teachings from Lord Krishna that are combinations of the above paths of yoga.

There are eighteen chapters (comprising 700 verses and 1400 lines) in the Bhagavad Gita. We will discuss only the key philosophically relevant verses from Chapter 2. Chapter 1 is mostly an introduction and is excluded for the sake of brevity. The spiritual seeker is highly encouraged to read the complete *Bhagavad Gita* to reap the benefits of the context and its wholehearted impact. The beauty of the *Bhagavad Gita* is its universal applicability to all of humanity from all walks of life, from the monks to the warriors to the householders.

CHAPTER 2: *SANKHYA YOGA* OR PATH OF 'ANALYTICAL' KNOWLEDGE

All eighteen chapters of the Gita end with the word yoga, which symbolizes the paths to achieving union with supreme reality. At a broad stroke, each chapter focuses on a specific path to attaining spiritual liberation or union with the divine. We must, however, note that most of these paths can be broadly categorized into Karma Yoga, Dhyana Yoga, Bhakti Yoga, and Jnana Yoga, as discussed before. These paths are consistent with the teachings of the *Upanishads* and the *Vedas*.

Some scholars point to Chapter 2 as the most important chapter of the *Bhagavad Gita* since it summarizes the teachings of the entire Gita. The word "Sankhya' means knowledge, and the analytical ideas and concepts of the second chapter bear some resemblance to the *Sankhya* school of Hindu philosophy that was discussed in earlier chapters. There are seventy-two verses in the second chapter, which begins with Lord Krishna delving straight into the very heart of the nature of the self (*Atman*). He then summarizes the key concepts of *Karma Yoga,* including duty, righteousness, and selfless action.

Krishna's teachings in the second chapter come in at the time when Arjuna, the warrior prince, has expressed emotional conflict about fighting the battle. Arjuna is grief-stricken and reluctant to engage in the battle with his own relatives, teachers, and friends. He decides to drop his weapon, and that's when Krishna's teachings to Arjuna begin.

NATURE OF THE SELF (VERSES 2.12 TO 2.30)

Lord Krishna teaches the immortality of the self (Atman) in these verses. We discussed the immortality of *Atman* in the *Upanishads,* and the Godhead Krishna reiterates that to Arjuna with insightful examples. He instructs Arjuna to think beyond the transient body (himself and the opposing army he needs to fight). A simple transliteration of the *shlokas* (verses) is given, and it is beyond the scope of his book to dive deeper into the individual verses. It is highly recommended that the reader reference a couple of well-known translations and analyses of the *Bhagavad Gita.* The **References** section can be consulted for some recommendations.

2.12

na tvēvāhaṃ jātu nāsaṃ na tvam nēmē janādhipāḥ |
na chaiva na bhaviṣyāmaḥ sarvē vayamataḥ param

Never was there a time when I did not exist, nor you, nor all these kings; nor in the future shall any of us cease to be.

2.13

dehino'smin yathaa dehe kaumaaram yauvanam jaraa tathaa
dehaantara praaptir dheeras tatra na mhuhyati

Just as in this body, the embodied self passes into childhood, youth, and old age, so also does he pass into another body; calm man does not grieve at it.

2.15

yam hi na vyathayantyete purusham purusharshabha samaduhkha
sukham dheeram so 'mritatwaaya kalpate

That calm man who remains unchanged in pain and pleasure, whom these cannot disturb, alone is able, O greatest among men, to attain immortality.

2.16

naasato vidyate bhaavo naabhaavo vidyate satah ubhayorapi
drishto'ntastwanayos tattwadarshibhih

The unreal has no existence. The Real never ceases to be (never ceases to exist). Men possessed of the knowledge of the Truth fully know both these.

This verse highlights the discernment needed to distinguish the real and the apparent (unreal). Anything that is transient, impermanent, ever-changing, like the body, mind, or intellect cannot be real, and the unchanging, infinite Atman never ceases to exist and is immortal.

2.17

avinaashi tu tad viddhi yena sarvam idam tatam vinaasham
avyayasyaasya na kaschit kartum arhati

Know `That' to be indestructible, by whom all this is pervaded. None can cause the destruction of That, the Imperishable.

The 'That' that is referred to in the verses above is the *Brahman* or the ultimate reality. It is also the Self (*Atman*) per Advaita Vedanta.

2.20

na jaayate mriyate vaa kadaachin naayam bhootwaa bhavitaa vaa na
bhooyah ajo nityah shaashwato'yam puraano na hanyate hanyamaane
shareere

He is never born, nor does He ever die; after having been, He again does not cease to be. Unborn, eternal, changeless and ancient. He is not killed when the body is killed.

The "He" in this verse is the true Self, which is changeless.

2.22

vaasaamsi jeernaani yathaa vihaaya navaani grihnaati naro'paraani
tathaa shareeraani vihaaya jeernaa nyanyaani samyaati navaani
dehee

Just as a man casts off his worn-out clothes and puts on new ones, so also the embodied Self casts off Its worn-out bodies and enters new ones. This verse highlights the indestructibility of the soul even amidst changing bodies. The word *'dehee'* in the above shloka signifies the jiva (individual person) made up of both the gross physical body and the subtle bodies, including the mind and intellect. Giving up the old body and assuming a new one, the *Atman* in the *Jiva*—the individual person—does not change.

The verse also underscores that by virtue of one's own *'karma'* (actions or deeds), the jiva becomes ready to assume a new body, leaving behind the old, worn-out body that has served its purpose. However, Vedanta explains that only the gross body dies, while the subtle and causal bodies do not. The subtle body, which encompasses the mental make-up of the person, is the core of every *jiva* and survives the death of the physical frame. In its next step of evolution, the jiva assumes a new physical frame. Throughout these transitions, the self, soul, or *Atman* remains unchanged. In reality, the soul, being immobile, does not migrate from one body to another; it is ever fixed, steady, and undergoes no change whatsoever.

2.24

acchedyo'yam adaahyo'yam akledyo'shoshya eva cha nityah
sarvagatah sthaanur achalo'yam sanaatanah

This Self cannot be cut, burnt, wetted, or dried up.

It is eternal, all-pervading, stable, ancient, and immovable.

2.25

avyakto'yam achintyo'yam avikaaryo'yam uchyate tasmaad evam
viditwainam naanushochitum arhasi

The Self is unmanifest, unthinkable, and unchangeable. Therefore, knowing it to be as such, you should not grieve.

The two verses above effectively prove that the Self is equivalent to Brahman, the ultimate reality

Due to the indestructibility of the Self, it is immortal.

Due to the Eternity of the Self, it transcends Time

Due to the All-pervading nature of the Self, it transcends Space

Due to the Manifestation of the Self, it transcends causality

This immortal, eternal, all-pervading Self can ONLY be

"the ONE without a second" (*Advaita*) and is *Brahman* (Ultimate reality)

2.30

dehee nityam avadhyo'yam dehe sarvasya bhaarata tasmaat sarvaani *bhootani na twam shochitum arhasi*

This Self, the indweller in the body of everyone, is always indestructible. O, Arjuna, therefore you should not grieve for any creature.

Lord Krishna thus concludes the teachings around profound *Upanishad* concepts, establishing the eternal nature of the soul and the finite nature of the body.

Moral Principles – Righteousness, Duty, Selfless Action

(Verses 2.31 to 2.53)

In these ensuing verses, Krishna gets down to ground reality, which has a universal appeal in contrast to the philosophical teachings covered in the previous verses.

2.31

swadharmam api chaavekshya na vikampitum arhasi dharmyaaddhi yuddhaachhreyo'nyat kshatriyasya na vidyate

Further, having regard to your duty (your own *Dharma*), you should not waver, for there is nothing higher for a Kshatriya than a righteous war.

The word '*Dharma*' has no literal translation in English but is a very important concept that the *Bhagavad Gita* preaches. In a broad sense, *Dharma* can mean Righteousness, Ethics, Duty, and Right Path. Most religions do encompass these principles and, hence, are universal in nature.

Sri Krishna has so far talked to Arjuna about the immortality of the Self and the perishable nature of the body to justify why he should fight. He now gives him moral reasons (*Dharma*) for fighting. He tells Arjuna that fighting is the natural duty of a *Kshatriya,* or "one born in the warrior class." His Dharma, as a warrior, needs him to engage in battle for upholding law, justice, and righteousness. Arjuna should, therefore, wage the war and ought not to waver from his duty.

Some Western critics take a dig at this verse, in particular, to falsely portray that Krishna is trying to incite violence or war. Nothing could be further from the truth, as the above verse simply illustrates that humanity needs to fulfill its duty (*Dharma*) which is moral, righteous, and ethical. It is immaterial whether you are a warrior, priest, doctor, engineer, plumber, or chef. Krishna preaches that *Dharma* requires you to fulfill your duty. The same applies to relationships in human society, be it with a father, mother, child, teacher, friend, mentor, or even a random stranger. Lord Krishna implies that everyone should discharge his or her duty very sincerely and enthusiastically, to the best of their power and ability, in whatever circumstances they are placed. That is the definition of Humanity with *Dharma.*

2.38

sukhaduhkhe same kritwaa laabhaalaabhau jayaajayau tato
yuddhaaya yujyaswa naivam paapamavaapsyasi

"Treating alike pleasure and pain, gain and loss, victory and defeat, engage in battle for the sake of the battle, thus you shall not incur sin."

The verse above is another gem from the teachings of the Gita. Fulfilling one's duty (*Dharma*) without attachment to the result of these actions. Selflessly executing one's *Dharma* is one of the key tenets of the Bhagavad Gita. Lord Krishna preaches equanimity in all challenging situations, whether it be pleasure or pain, gain or loss, victory or defeat. This is a profound lesson from the Gita. Pleasure and pain are two sides of the same coin; one cannot exist without the other, and the realization of this is critical to leading a blissful life. This ensures success in life and enables the elimination of the human ego and desires. Equanimity involves detachment from the ego, and this kind of righteous, selfless living results in enduring happiness.

In the ensuing verses, Lord Krishna delves into *Karma Yoga* as a means for liberation and bliss. *Karma Yoga* is the path of action. He summarizes *Karma Yoga* as engaging in action without any attachment to the result of such action. This is also termed *nishkama karma* (selfless action). Once anyone engages in an action with a motive or desire, it results in attachment to the results, which results in losing the equanimity of the mind regardless of the results. *Karma Yoga* is considered a preparatory step for the purification of the mind before engaging in higher forms of Yoga, like *Jnana Yoga, Dhyana* Yoga, or *Bhakti Yoga*. Karma Yogis develop a level of selflessness in their everyday actions, which purifies the mind for higher spiritual realization.

2.40

nehaabhikramanaasho 'sti pratyavaayo na vidyate swalpamapyasya dharmasya traayate mahato bhayaat

In this way, no effort is ever lost and no harm is ever done. Even very little of this discipline (*Dharma*) saves a man from the Great Fear.

Lord Krishna praises the merits of *Karma Yoga* in the verse above.

2.47

If there's one verse that decks the halls of homes and buildings of millions of Hindus worldwide, it's the above. It is perhaps the most famous and widely used phrase from the *Bhagavad Gita*, where Krishna advises the importance of selfless action.

karmanyevaadhikaaraste maa phaleshu kadaachana

maa karmaphalahetur bhoor maa te sango 'stwakarmani

"Your right is to work only, but never to claim its fruits.

Do not become an instrument for making your actions yield fruit, nor let your attachment be to inaction."

If you decipher this carefully, Lord Krishna is advising what the West calls 'Mindfulness'. The advice is to be completely mindful and engaged in the action without desiring or attaching to the results. It is action for the sake of Dharma (duty) as long as it is righteous and moral. The non-attachment to results frees the mind from bondage and purifies the mind as well as the heart. This is the core of the above verse.

Lord Krishna also emphasizes that inaction is not an option, to quell the misconception that inaction is better than action with attachments. This is a crucial teaching where humanity is advised to engage in action according to the respective Dharma and strive to eliminate the laggard, lethargic, slothful traits of inaction.

2.48

Yogasthah kuru karmani sangam tyaktwaa dhananjaya.

siddhyasiddhyoh samo bhootwaa samatwam yoga uchyate

"Perform your actions, O Dhananjaya (Arjuna), being established in or integrated with Yoga,

abandoning attachment and remaining even minded both in success and failure. This evenness of mind is called Yoga."

Lord Krishna refers to *Karma Yoga* when he means Yoga in the verse above. Krishna reemphasizes the equanimity of mind, which was discussed in the earlier verses, and that poise in mind can only happen if one does not succumb to the temporal emotions in life. As has been said, there can be no life without death, no happiness without sadness, no win without a loss, and no pleasure without pain. Only equanimity or bliss, as has been discussed in *Vedanta,* is unparalleled as being enduring or eternal. That is the term that is used interchangeably as Nirvana (Buddhism), Moksha (Hinduism), self-realization (Monistic religions), God-realization (Theistic religions).

In the verse above, Lord Krishna gives very practical advice for all of humanity on how *Karma Yoga* can be used in everyday life to attain equanimity of the mind, which then prepares the mind for higher forms of self-realization.

In the next few verses, Krishna reiterates how the practice of *Karma Yoga* in everyday life leads to liberation.

2.49

doorena hyavaram karma buddhiyogaad dhananjaya

buddhau sharanamanwiccha kripanaah phalahetavah

"O Arjuna, far inferior, indeed, is mere action, to action performed with evenness of mind. Seek refuge in this evenness. Wretched are they who work for results."

2.50

buddhiyukto jahaateeha ubhe sukrita dushkrite

tasmaad yogaaya yujyaswa yogah karmasu kaushalam

"Endowed with evenness of mind, one casts off in this very life both good and evil deeds. Therefore, devote yourself to Yoga (of equanimity); skill in action lies in the practice of this Yoga."

2.51

karmajam buddhiyuktaa hi phalam tyaktwaa maneeshinah

janmabandha vinirmuktaah padam gacchantyanaamayam

"The wise, possessed of equanimity, having abandoned the fruits of their actions and being freed from the fetters of birth, attain the state that is beyond all evil (reaches the blissful supreme state)."

2.52

yadaa te mohakalilam buddhir vyatitarishyati

tadaa gantaasi nirvedam shrotavyasya shrutasya cha

"When your mind crosses beyond the mire of delusion, then you shall achieve indifference regarding things already heard and things yet to be heard (about enjoyments of this world or the next)."

The 'delusion' that Lord Krishna refers to is the non-discrimination between Self and non-Self. Falsely identifying the Self with the body through the external senses and the mind through various desires and attachments leads one to be devoid of eternal bliss. Only when purity of mind is attained through the sincere practice of Karma Yoga can one transcend the senses (things that are heard) and beyond the senses (things yet to be heard).

2.53

shrutivipratipannaa te yadaa sthaasyati nishchalaa

samaadhaavachalaa buddhistadaa yogam avaapsyasi

"When your mind, now perplexed by what you have heard, stands firm and steady in the Self, then you will have attained Yoga or Self-Realization."

The mind gets agitated due to the continuous stimuli it receives from the external world through the sense organs. When an individual, in spite of such disturbances and agitations of the mind, does not lose his cool, inner serenity, and equipoise and remains concentrated in the knowledge of the self, he is considered to have attained yoga, samadhi, or *self-realization*.

This is the first time Lord Krishna invokes the word *samadhi* as the ultimate pedestal in the quest for spiritual liberation. *Samadhi* is the Vedantic term that we discussed earlier and is the highest kind of consciousness wherein the object with which the mind is in communion is the Divine Self which is the result of the discrimination between the Self and the Non-Self, the Real and the Unreal.

Lord Krishna advises that Karma Yoga involves faithfully following his *Dharma* (duty) and engaging in *Nishkama Karma* (selfless action). He then develops a pure mind and heart, which prepares him for true knowledge of the self and is considered to have attained self-realization.

Knowledge, Self-Realization (Verses 2.54 to 2.72)

The last eighteen verses are packed with a summary of attaining self-realization, including step-by-step guidance. Arjuna, intrigued by the state of *samadhi,* or eternal bliss, asks Krishna the following:

"What is the description of him who has steady wisdom and is merged in the superconscious state (Samadhi)? How does one of steady wisdom speak? How does he sit? How does he walk?"

Lord Krishna's responses, captured below, conclude this epic chapter. These verses are of extraordinary significance as Krishna answers a question that all of humanity has been asking for a long time: 'What is true wisdom, and how can one achieve this wisdom to become a wise man?"

2.55

prajahaati yadaa kaamaan sarvaan paartha manogataan
atmanyevaatmanaa tushtah sthitaprajnastadochyate

"When a man completely casts off all the desires of the mind, his Self, finding satisfaction in itself alone, then he is called a man of steady wisdom."

The verse above answers the question about the end goal of any kind of Yoga, like Karma Yoga, as an example. Engaging in selfless action, following one's duties, and purifying the mind and heart are all preparatory, per the earlier discussion. 'Preparation for what? you might ask, and the answer lies in the verse above. When one discovers happiness in oneself by oneself, then he is said to have attained wisdom. The goal is deep self-inquiry to discover your true self. When one finds happiness in the self, he does not depend on external objects or desires for happiness.

Vedanta teachings prove that our inner Self or Atman, is itself inner bliss (*Ananda*), and our goal is to actually realize this blissful state through knowledge, devotion, or selfless action.

In the next few verses, Lord Krishna teaches the characteristics of the person who has attained this steady wisdom.

2.56

duhkheshwanudwignamanaah sukheshu vigatasprihah
veetaraagabhayakrodhah sthitadheer munir uchyate

"He whose mind is not shaken by adversity, who does not hanker after pleasures and who is free from attachment, fear and anger, is called a sage of steady wisdom."

2.57

yah sarvatraanabhisnehas tattat praapya shubhaashubham

naabhinandati na dweshti tasya prajnaa pratishthitaa

"He who is not attached to anything, who neither rejoices nor is, vexed when he obtains good or evil – his wisdom is firmly fixed."

The above verse highlights 'detachment' and should not be construed as escaping the experience that is life. It only means maintaining the equanimity of the mind during life's ups and downs and always being engaged in action. This can only happen when we treat the pleasures and pains of life exactly the same way.

Lord Krishna then explains that detachment can only happen by controlling the outward senses, and the following verses highlight the importance of sense control.

2.59

vishayaa vinivartante niraahaarasya dehinah

rasavarjam raso 'pyasya param drishtwaa nivartate

"The objects of the senses fall away from the abstinent man but not the taste for them. But even the taste falls away when the Supreme is seen"

The Lord explains the subtle difference between outer detachment and inner detachment. As an example, if the outward senses are controlled but a desire for these objects exists in the mind, this really defeats the purpose of true detachment. Thus, it is important to have complete renunciation and detachment in both the body (outer senses) and the mind (absence of desires). This can only happen if the mind is single-pointedly focused on the self or God-realization.

2.61

taani sarvaani samyamya yukta aaseeta matparah

vashe hi yasyendriyaani tasya prajnaa pratishthitaa

"Having restrained all the senses, he should sit steadfast, intent on Me; his wisdom is steady whose senses are under control."

This verse highlights the need for deep meditation on the Lord. The 'Me' here can be construed as the Lord Krishna himself in the form of incarnation of God (*Saguna Brahman*) or the monistic way of meditating on the formless Brahman, the ultimate reality. Part IV explains practical meditation techniques that can be highly personalized for the individual seeker.

2.62, 2.63

In the following verses, Krishna advises Arjuna of the perils of yielding to sense objects and desires.

dhyaayato vishayaan pumsah sangas teshoopajaayate

sangaat sanjaayate kaamah kaamaat krodho 'bhijaayate

"When a man thinks of objects, attachment for them arises; from attachment, desire is born; from desire arises anger."

krodhaad bhavati sammohah sammohaat smriti vibhramah

smritibhramshaad buddhinaasho buddhinaashaat pranashyati

"From anger comes delusion, from delusion the loss of memory, from the loss of memory the destruction of intelligence; from the destruction of intelligence, he perishes."

2.70, 2.71, and 2.72

These verses highlight the state of the realized man.

"aapooryamaanam achalapratishtham

samudram aapah pravishanti yadwat

 tadwat kaamaa yam pravishanti sarve

sa shaantim aapnoti na kaamakaami"

"He attains peace into whom all desires enter as the waters enter the ocean, which is full to the brim and grounded in stillness, but not the man who is the desirer of desires."

Lord Krishna poetically explains the equanimity of mind as akin to a massive ocean that is not at all affected by the waters flowing into it from all sides. Similarly, an enlightened person is not affected by external sense objects and desires. Such an individual who maintains true peace in spite of being a target for the stimuli conveyed through his sense organs by innumerable sense objects is a man of enlightenment. He who looks outside for enjoyment never attains peace.

vihaaya kaamaan yah sarvaan pumaamshcharati nihsprihah nirmamo nirahankaarah sa shaantim adhigacchati

"That man attains peace who, abandoning all desires, moves about without longing, devoid of the sense of `I'-ness and `my'-ness."

The chapters in Part II and Part IV expand on the concept of achieving this I-lessness, completely devoid of human ego, as the principal method to achieve self-realization. Lord Krishna states that peace or bliss is only achievable with a selfless mindset devoid of desires for external sense objects.

eshaa braahmee sthitih paartha nainaam praapya vimuhyati sthitwaasyaamantakaale'pi brahmanirvaanamricchati

"This is the Brahmi-state, O Son of Pritha. Attaining this, none is deluded. Being established therein, even at the hour of death, one attains final liberation in Brahman."

The Lord mentions a state of union with the Brahman, or moksha (liberation), as the *Brahmi*-state. This state is filled with utter bliss, and a man in this state will never fall into delusion. This state, as has been propounded in the previous verse, can only happen when the individual ego ends and a true self emerges. This true self is what *Vedanta* refers to as *Sat* (existence), *Chit* (consciousness), and *Ananda* (bliss)..

This concludes Chapter 2 and is arguably the most important chapter of the Bhagavad Gita, as Lord Krishna begins with a deep philosophical inquiry into the eternal Atman and concludes with practical techniques to achieve inner bliss, which are universally applicable through knowledge (Jnana) and selfless action involving renunciation and detachment (Karma), Meditation, and devotion (Dhyana and Bhakti).

Chapters 3 through 18 are not covered in this book, where the Lord delves into various aspects of Karma Yoga, Bhakti Yoga, Dhyana Yoga, and Jnana Yoga for self-realization.

PART II

NEO VEDANTA

Chapter 6

INTRODUCTION TO NEO VEDANTA

Neo Vedanta encompasses a modern interpretation of the teachings of Advaita Vedanta for the contemporary audience and emerged in the late 19th and early 20th century. Neo Vedanta aimed to make Vedanta more relevant and compatible with significant scientific advancements of that era. It was also influenced by Western philosophical and scientific ideas, seeking to bridge the gap between Eastern and Western thought.

Prominent figures such as Swami Vivekananda, Swami Ramakrishna Paramahamsa (Guru of Swami Vivekananda), Swami Dayanand Saraswati, and Sri Aurobindo propagated Vedanta in a more inclusive and universal manner worldwide. These great scholars and philosophers aimed to foster a sense of unity through Vedanta that transcended the sectarian boundaries prevalent in India during the era of British Colonialism.

One of the unique aspects of these Neo Vedanta pioneers is their emphasis on the practical application of Vedanta through selfless social service and the upliftment of poverty prevalent in society.

One of the real inspirations for me and many across the globe is Swami Vivekananda. He stands as a towering figure as a saint, philosopher, theologian, poet, among other roles, and is largely responsible for the massive impact of Hinduism and Advaita Vedanta in the Western world. Swami Vivekananda was one of the early pioneers in using the Western playbook of communication and outreach to propagate Vedanta and Hinduism. He spread its message globally through books, lectures, and various media. Swami Vivekananda's address at the Parliament of the World's Religions in Chicago (1893) is a notable event representing this aspect.

We will exclusively focus on Swami Vivekananda in this section on Neo Vedanta due to his enormous contributions and the countless impact he continues to have on humanity.

Vivekananda in Chicago, September 1893. On the Left note, Vivekananda wrote: "One infinite pure and holy — beyond thought beyond qualities I bow down to thee".[1]

Swami Vivekananda was born as Narendranath Datta on January 12, 1863, in Calcutta, which was then the capital of British India. Swami was a passionate reader, and owing to his deep interest in Hindu mythology and scriptures, he read the famous epics Ramayana, Mahabharata, Vedas, Upanishads, and Bhagavad Gita at a very young age. He was also a sports enthusiast and took an active part in physical exercise.

At an adolescent age, he opposed idol worship and believed in Nirguna Brahman (a formless god) shaped by his association with Brahmo Samaj, a modern Hindu philosophical system that opposed any ritualistic belief system and was more rational and scientific.

During his college days, he came to know about Sri Ramakrishna, the mystical and god-like saint from Dakshineshwar that everyone was talking about. At first, he did not believe in Sri Ramakrishna's mysticism, ideologies, or Advaita Vedanta. After a life-changing experience involving his rendezvous with Sri Ramakrishna, Swami Vivekananda accepted him as the guru, his spiritual teacher, and became his most notable and famous disciple.

In 1886, after Sri Ramakrishna passed away, a young 23-year-old named Naren took the monastic vow, became a *sannyasi* (monk), and came to be known as Swami Vivekananda. During the next 7 years until 1893, Swami Vivekananda traveled extensively inside India as a wandering monk, sleeping in parks and public places. During his travels, he met the diverse diaspora of India and different cultures, grew empathetic toward the struggle in the mostly poor and downtrodden India, and aimed to uplift society from this sorrow and misery. Swami's story is very similar to that of Gautama the Buddha, who renunciated his kingly throne and pleasures after seeing the struggles and unhappiness in society.

In 1893, Swami Vivekananda began his first voyage aboard, traveling to China, Japan, Canada, and eventually Chicago in the United States. September 11, 1893, is a very consequential date as Swami Vivekananda represented India and spoke about Hinduism and Vedanta for the first time to a Western audience in the World Parliament of Religions.

His brilliant oratorial skills and inclusive tone brought the audience to stand still, and he received a standing ovation. His opening line from the speech "Brothers and Sisters of America" is still remembered as one of the greatest speeches ever given in any setting.

In the ensuing days and months, he wrote numerous papers and gave numerous speeches on Vedanta, Hinduism, and the need for full inclusivity and a universal brotherhood approach to religions. His speeches and addresses had an immediate effect not just on America but on the entire world. He became a hero, a celebrity, and, in no time, the "greatest figure in the parliament of world religions."

Swami spent the next two years traveling across the United States, delivering lectures and speeches. In 1894, he established the Vedanta Society of New York. Some of his famous listeners included Albert Einstein, Nikola Tesla, and other famous scientific luminaries who were fascinated by the profound philosophy of Swami's lectures.

He also visited the United Kingdom in 1895 and 1896 and various European countries.

Swami Vivekananda expanded the Vedantic classification of the yoga system for the modern audience. They are:

From the *Vedanta* school of Hinduism

Karma Yoga: Yoga of selfless action and righteousness

Bhakti Yoga: Yoga of supreme devotion to personal God

Jnana Yoga: Yoga of Knowledge of the Absolute

From the yoga school (influenced by Patanjali's yoga sutras)

Raja Yoga: Yoga of Meditation

Swami Vivekananda also set up the Ramakrishna mission and Ramakrishna Math in 1897 at Belur Math, a lasting legacy for his beloved guru Sri Ramakrishna Paramahamsa and to spread the message of Advaita Vedanta.

On July 4, 1902, Swami Vivekananda awoke early, went to the monastery at Belur Math, and meditated for three hours. He taught the Upanishads, Sanskrit grammar, and the philosophy of yoga to his students. It is said that late in the evening, Swami Vivekananda went to his room, asking not to be disturbed, and he passed away that night while meditating.

According to his disciples, Vivekananda attained *Mahasamadhi*.

Mahasamadhi refers to the conscious and intentional act of leaving one's physical body at the time of death by individuals who have attained a high-level of spiritual realization or mastery over their mind and body. It is considered a voluntary and controlled exit from the physical realm, often referred to as a conscious and deliberate departure. Vivekananda fulfilled his prophecy that he would not live forty years, which indicated that his departure was a conscious and intentional act.

Chapter 7

INFLUENTIAL WORKS OF SWAMI VIVEKANANDA

Swami Vivekananda can only be known through his works. He was a powerful orator and writer in English and Bengali, and most of his published works were compiled from lectures given around the world, which were "mainly delivered impromptu and with little preparation. His main work involves lectures on all four yoga systems (Karma, Bhakti, Jnana, and Raja).

Unlike the Great Acharyas of *Vedanta* (Shankaracharya, Ramanujacharya, and Madhvacharya), he did not write an elaborate commentary on the Upanishads or Bhagavad Gita but focused on the practical application of these ancient Vedantic systems to all of humanity in an inclusive and contemporary way. He emphasized the universality of truth and the acceptance of diverse paths to reach it.

His monistic views, influenced by the Advaita Vedanta, played a major role in introducing the Vedanta philosophies to the West. It is solely because of him that Hinduism gained the status of a major world religion.

He played a crucial role in the Indian Nationalistic Renaissance, reigniting a sense of pride in Indian culture, philosophy, and spirituality at a time when India was grappling with colonialism and its aftermath.

According to social reformer Charles Freer Andrews, "The Swami's intrepid patriotism gave a new color to the national movement throughout India. More than any other single individual of that period,

Vivekananda had made his contribution to the new awakening of India." His nationalistic ideas influenced many Indian thinkers and leaders. Sri Aurobindo (a renowned Indian theologian and philosopher) regarded Vivekananda as the one who awakened India spiritually.

The father of the Indian freedom struggle, Mahatma Gandhi, had heartfelt admiration for Swami's practical application of the Vedanta and said, "Who has maintained this Hindu religion in a state of splendor by cutting down the dead wood of tradition?"

The reader is highly encouraged to possess one of the greatest gems in spiritual history, "The Complete Works," which is a collection of his writings, lectures, and discourses in nine volumes.

His teachings can be summarized in this amazing quote.

"Each soul is potentially divine. The goal is to manifest this divinity within by controlling nature, both external and internal.

Do this either by work, or worship, or mental discipline, or philosophy—by one, or more, or all of these—and be free. This is the whole of religion. Doctrines, or dogmas, or rituals, or books, or temples, or forms, are but secondary details."

Work here refers to *karma yoga*, worship refers to *bhakti yoga*, mental discipline refers to *raja yoga,* and philosophy refers to *jnana yoga.* This universal message appeals to humanity as a whole, from the poor, the illiterate, and the impoverished to the masters and scholars of philosophy and science.

In the next few sections, we will extract some of the gems of the "complete works" structured across the four yoga techniques.

Chapter 8

KEY DIFFERENCES BETWEEN ADI SHANKARACHARYA'S ADVAITA VEDANTA & SWAMI VIVEKANANDA'S TEACHINGS

Swami Vivekananda's teachings were mostly based on the oneness and non-dual nature propagated by the Advaita Vedanta. However, it is important for the reader to understand the subtle and signature changes that were part of Swami Vivekananda's teachings.

Swami Vivekananda came almost 1100 years after Adi Shankara. Early 20th-century India was a very complex period in India, both politically and economically. There was a freedom struggle from British colonialism, rampant poverty throughout India, and Western philosophical influence in Indian theology, among other things.

These socio-economic factors significantly influenced Swami Vivekananda to tweak or morph the timeless Upanishadic teachings for the modern age. Swami was also significantly influenced by inclusivity and multi-cultural influence through his guru, Ramakrishna Paramahamsa. Swami Vivekananda transformed the timeless wisdom in the Advaita Vedanta into something more relevant to the modern age.

+ He stressed more selfless service (*seva*) to humanity as a key aspect of spiritual realization. The Advaita Vedanta philosophy was more focused on spiritual realization through self-inquiry (Jnana Yoga).

- His teachings were more for all of humanity (the masses). Meanwhile, Advaita Vedanta mostly focused on the individual's ability to achieve Brahman through philosophical inquiry.

- His teachings were simple enough for common people to grasp and needed no expertise in *Sanskrit* or the philosophical mindset that forms the tenets of some Upanishadic scriptures.

- Integration of Karma Yoga (Action & Duty) as well as Bhakti Yoga (devotion to personal God) into Jnana Yoga, while traditional Advaita Vedanta focuses primarily on Jnana Yoga.

Swami Vivekananda understood that most of the poor, downtrodden masses in late 19th-century India did not have the means to imbibe the deep philosophical concepts of self-inquiry in the Upanishads. At the same time, he recognized the enormous love and devotion of various personal gods that had existed at that time and are still a part of the vibrant Hindu religion.

Chapter 9

KARMA YOGA FROM THE VIEWPOINT OF SWAMI VIVEKANANDA

Swami Vivekananda elucidates the concept of 'Karma' as work and action in everyday life. Everything we do, both physical and mental, is *karma* and leaves a mark on us. All the actions or work, whether good or bad, small or big, are tied simply to the display of thought, the manifestation of the will of the man. He gives the example of great men like Buddha and Jesus, and the enormous will that they possessed could not possibly be hereditary but only be accumulated over several life cycles attributed to Karma.

"Everything in the world is the manifestation of the will of man;

The will of the man is caused by character.

Character is manufactured by Karma."

"As is karma, so is the manifestation of the will," writes Swami Vivekananda in the chapter on Karma Yoga.

His fundamental teaching of karma yoga was heavily influenced by the Bhagavad Gita and urges people to commit to actions without selfishness. He truly believes that once a man becomes perfectly unselfish and has transcended the "I-ness," he merges with the divine.

He gives an example of an ideal of Karma Yoga with this example.

"The ideal man is he who, in the midst of the greatest silence and solitude, finds the intensest activity, and in the midst of the intensest activity, finds the silence and solitude of the desert."

This is very similar to the following quote from Lord Sri Krishna in Chapter 4 of the *Bhagavad Gita*.

कर्मण्यकर्म यः पश्येदकर्मणि च कर्म यः।

स बुद्धिमान्मनुष्येषु स युक्तः कृत्स्नकर्मकृत्।।

Karmaṇy akarma yaḥ paśhyed akarmaṇi cha karma yaḥ

Sa buddhimān manuṣhyeṣhu sa yuktaḥ kṛitsna-karma-kṛit

"He who sees inaction in action, and action in inaction, he is intelligent among men, and he is in the transcendental position, although engaged in all kinds of work"

Apart from selfless action, Swami Vivekananda also stressed that individuals could attain a sense of freedom and inner peace through,

Renunciation – renouncing the fruits of their actions.

Detachment – from the outcomes of actions

Inspired by the Vedantic teachings, Swami Vivekananda taught that Discipline is a key aspect of Karma Yoga. He encouraged individuals to cultivate focus and discipline.

Swami Vivekananda also dedicated an entire chapter on "duty" and stressed that fulfilling one's duty and responsibilities in society is a vital aspect of Karma Yoga. He taught one to perform one's duties diligently and selflessly for the betterment of society, which ultimately leads to attaining the spiritual path.

Swami Vivekananda's interpretation of Karma Yoga is largely absent in the Upanishads (Sruti) but is borrowed heavily from the *Bhagavad Gita* (Smriti) and is more easily palatable by most of humanity. His teachings encourage living beings to lead a life of selfless and continuous action, detachment from the results of the action, performing one's duties diligently, having a purpose, and having strong discipline where every day work becomes a means to spiritual growth and fulfillment. That is *Karma Yoga*!

Chapter 10

BHAKTI YOGA FROM THE VIEWPOINT OF SWAMI VIVEKANANDA

Swami Vivekananda describes *Bhakti* as a "real, genuine search after the Lord, a search beginning, continuing, and ending in love." He also quotes some of the aphorisms from some of the sages that are based solely on *Bhakti,* and these aphorisms proclaim that Bhakti is an "intense love for god" and higher than other forms of yoga as it transcends all worldly objects. He also proclaims that of the four yogas, which are the paths to liberation (Karma, Bhakti, Raja, and Jnana), Bhakti is the "easiest and most natural way to reach the divine."

Swami Vivekananda gives us a beautiful example of essential things for a bird to do to fly and achieve liberation.

Yoga for liberation

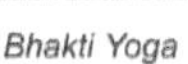

Swami Vivekananda also dispels the popular myth that *Jnana Yoga* and *Bhakti Yoga* are inherently different. We have read in the previous chapters that Advaita Vedanta (Monism) focuses more on the Jnana Yoga through self-inquiry to achieve unity with the Nirguna Brahman (formless and attribute-less Brahman). On the contrary, and although an oversimplification, Dvaita and Visishtadvaita Vedanta (monotheistic) emphasize Bhakti (devotion and love) to *Ishvara* or *Saguna Brahman* (the supreme deity with attributes) to achieve liberation or moksha. According to Swami, the Jnanis (those who practice Jnana Yoga) hold Bhakti to be an instrument of liberation, while the Bhaktas (those who practice Bhakti Yoga) look upon this as the instrument and the thing to be attained. This can also be construed as lower and higher forms of worship, each leading to the same supreme liberation. These can be summarized by the visual below.

Swami Vivekananda summarizes Bhakti and Jnana Yoga interdependence as "with perfect love (Bhakti), true knowledge (Jnana) is bound to come even unsought, and thus from perfect knowledge (Jnana), true love (Bhakti) is inseparable."

Swami Vivekananda also uses quotes from the Upanishads and the great sages (Maha Acharyas) to unravel the true meaning of Bhakti.

Importance of Yoga - Monism & Monotheism

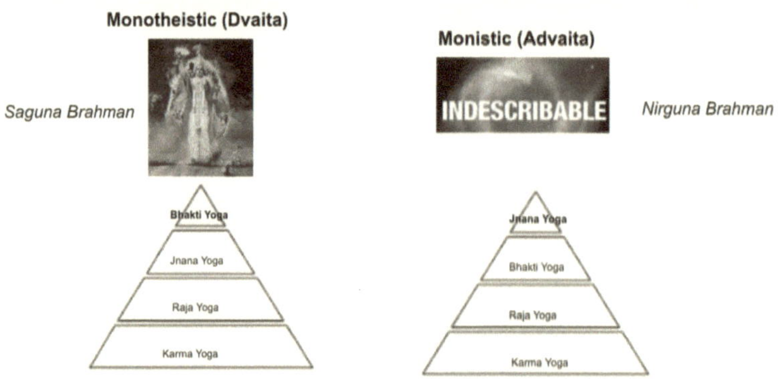

"Sort of Bhakti, in which, without seeking results, such as sense-enjoyments, etc., all works are dedicated to that Teacher of Teachers, the Supreme Lord."

"That deathless love which the ignorant have for the fleeting objects of senses—as I keep meditating upon Thee (supreme Lord Ishvara)—may not that love slip away from my heart."

Bhakti is, therefore, a series of mental efforts at religious realization, beginning with ordinary worship (that may involve rituals) and ending in a supreme intensity of love for Ishvara (the personal god or Saguna Brahman).

Swami Vivekananda also answers the perplexing question that has led to various debates among Vedantic scholars on whether the supreme reality (Brahman) is a personal God (Ishvara) or Nirguna Brahman (formless). He says the God of Love of the Bhakta and the "Sat-chit-Ananda" (Existence-Consciousness-Bliss) aspect of Brahman of the Jnani are ONE AND THE SAME.

Swami Vivekananda says, "All is Brahman and is one without a second; only the Brahman, as unity or absolute, is too much an abstraction to be loved and worshipped; so the Bhakta chooses the 'relative' aspect of the Brahman, that is, Ishvara, the Supreme Ruler." He also gives an example to illustrate the above theory.

"Brahman is the clay of substance out of which an infinite variety of articles are fashioned. As clay, they are all one, but the form or manifestation differentiates them. Before every one of them was made, they all existed potentially in clay, and of course, they are identical substantially; but when formed, and so long as form remains, they are separate and different." He also states that the personal god, or Ishvara, is the highest form of reality that "the human mind can comprehend."

This theory of unity in diversity of names and forms is directly taken from the Advaita Vedanta propounded by Shankaracharya. Swami Vivekananda strikes a balance between the monistic and monotheistic views of religion, still holding to the fundamental *Advaitic* view of the oneness of the Brahman.

CHAPTER 11

RAJA YOGA FROM THE VIEWPOINT OF SWAMI VIVEKANANDA

The term Raja Yoga (Yoga of the Royal Path) was coined by Swami Vivekananda and is more "experiential" in nature than the other forms of yoga. Raja Yoga is completely based on Sage Patanjali's Yoga sutras (which we covered extensively in the Yoga system of philosophy). Swami Vivekananda moves beyond the Vedanta school to the Yoga school of Hinduism to adopt Raja Yoga as one of the paths for spiritual liberation. Raja Yoga (like the Yoga sutras of Patanjali) emphasizes control of the mind and contains the Ashtanga (8 limbs) as a means to attain liberation.

A spiritual seeker wants the truth and wants to experience it himself. Swami Vivekananda quotes the Vedas: "When a man has grasped the truth, realized the truth, felt the truth within his hearts of hearts, then alone would all doubts vanish, and all darkness is scattered, and all crookedness made straight". This method of experiencing truth for yourself is the essence of Raja Yoga.

Swami Vivekananda terms Raja Yoga a science, and this method proposes a practical and scientifically worked-out method of reaching the ultimate truth. The science of Raja Yoga emphasizes observing the internal states of the mind itself. Raja Yoga calls for turning the mind inside, stopping it from going outside, and then concentrating all its powers and throwing them upon the mind itself so that it knows its own nature. Swami Vivekananda proclaims that this is the only way to scientifically approach this subject. The scientific aspect of this yoga really begins with the 'observation' first. He then explains the end result of such an 'internal' observation of the mind, which is to gain knowledge.

"When by observing and analyzing his own mind, man comes face-to-face, as it were with something which is never destroyed, something which is by its own nature eternally pure and perfect, he will no longer be miserable, no more unhappy."

Raja Yoga also emphasizes deep 'concentration' as a method to attain this knowledge. It is necessary to study the mind and, in a bit more abstract sense, the mind studying the mind. The goal of Raja Yoga is to explicitly detail how to concentrate the mind and how to discover the innermost secrets in our minds, leading us to the basis of genuine religion. The beauty of Raja Yoga is that no faith or belief is necessary as a pre-requisite. Just like pure science, believe nothing until you have experienced it yourself. The study of Raja Yoga takes a long time and constant practice.

The Raja Yoga has been borrowed from the Yoga Sutras of Patanjali and follows the Ashtanga (8 limbs) to achieve liberation. The Ashtanga are Yama, Niyama, Asana, Pranayama, Dharana, Dhyana, and Samadhi. We will only discuss Samadhi in this chapter as Swami Vivekananda shares deep insights into this state. The reader can refer to the early introduction chapters that discussed the first seven steps of Ashtanga Yoga.

Swami Vivekananda explains the three planes of consciousness to clearly shed light on the distinctive state of *samadhi*. He states, "When a man goes into Samadhi, he goes into it a fool and comes out a sage."

Planes of Consciousness

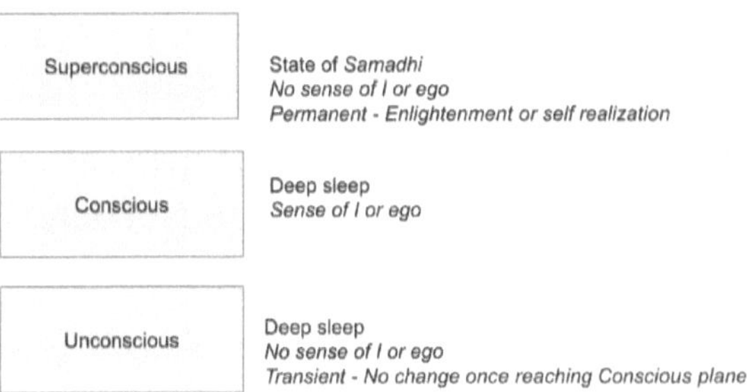

The goal of Raja Yoga is to experience that "the mind itself has a higher state of existence, beyond reason, a superconscious state, and when the mind gets to a higher state, then this knowledge, beyond reasoning, comes to man. Metaphysical and transcendental knowledge come to that man."

As humans, we are trained to think that the conscious mind can do everything, while the *yogis* who reached the *Samadhi* state experienced a higher state of superconsciousness that transcended the mind. This state is completely unselfish, with the feeling of 'I-ness' completely disappearing. The yogi in the state of Samadhi is said to experience union with the divine, losing all the distinction between subject and object. Samadhi is a highly advanced state of meditation and spiritual realization and is considered one of the highest states of consciousness in the yogic and Vedantic traditions.

Swami Vivekananda, his Guru Ramakrishna Paramahamsa, Paramahamsa Yogananda, and Ramana Maharshi are some of the divine yogis who have attained the state of *Nirvikalpa Samadhi*, a state of deep meditation and self-realization.

Swami says, "the very fact that one man can reach this state, proves that it is possible for every man to do so. Not only is it possible, but every man must, eventually, get to that state, and that is religion. Experience is the only teacher we have."

There is no shortcut to achieving this state of superconsciousness. All eight steps outlined in the Raja Yoga (Patanjali's Yoga Sutras) have to be followed. If the mind is able to concentrate on an object for extended periods of time and eventually dwell only on the internal part of the perception of which the object was the effect, everything comes under the control of such a mind.

Raja Yoga, like the other forms of yoga (Karma, Bhakti, and Jnana), highlights selflessness, egolessness, or I-lessness as the cornerstone of achieving spiritual liberation. Raja Yoga claims, "As long as there is desire, there is no happiness'.

Swami Vivekananda concludes, "Each one of these steps to attain Samadhi has been reasoned out, properly adjusted, scientifically organized, and, when faithfully practiced, will surely lead us to the desired end. Then will all sorrows cease, all miseries vanish; the seeds for actions will be burned, and the soul will be free forever."

Chapter 12

JNANA YOGA FROM THE VIEWPOINT OF SWAMI VIVEKANANDA

Swami Vivekananda's true calling life was *Jnana Yoga*, and he has extensively lectured about *Jnana Yoga* in the West (United Kingdom and United States). The complete works of Swami Vivekananda used as a reference in this section are based on transcriptions of his lectures in the West.

RELIGION

Swami Vivekananda finds a common thread in all religions: that the human mind, at certain moments, can transcend the senses and the power of reasoning. These moments produce facts, and they form the basis of all religions. similar to the *rishis* (sages) who, in a deep meditative state of mind, wrote the Vedas. Swami argues that a supersensuous state is needed and that it is NOT possible to propound these religious ideas in a normal sensory and reason-based environment.

The output of these religious proclamations is abstract and infinite, such as an omnipresent being, a personal Omniscient God, or a Moral Law. These are the highest ideals that a human strives to achieve, whether it is infinite pleasure or infinite power. The biggest mistake humans make is trying to realize this infinite ideal with a finite body and mind.

Swami Vivekananda gives two essential definitions of religion.

"This conquering of the inner man, understanding the secrets of the subtle workings that are within the human mind, and knowing its wonderful secrets, belong entirely to religion."

"Religion as a science, as a study, is the greatest and healthiest exercise that the human mind can have. This pursuit of the infinite, this struggle to grasp the infinite, this effort to get beyond the limitations of the senses," he concludes by saying that this struggle is the grandest and most glorious that man can make.

THE REAL NATURE OF MAN

In this chapter, Swami offers a lucidly logical explanation of what the soul (*Atman*) is, corroborating the *Advaita Vedanta* view.

Atman has neither shape nor form, and hence is omnipresent. Atman is beyond the mind, and most religious scriptures agree on the above two characteristics of *Atman*. The concepts of time, space, and causation are all in the mind, and if the *Atman* is beyond the mind, then it is beyond the realm of time, space, and causation, and hence infinite. By logical reasoning, infinite cannot be two and can ONLY be 'one without a second' (*Advaita*).

If Atman (soul) is infinite, there can only be one soul, and the idea of each individual having their own soul cannot be real. The Real Man says Swami Vivekananda is 'one and infinite' and is the 'omnipresent spirit'. He also introduces the term 'Apparent Man' as the limitation of this 'Real Man'.

In essence, Swami Vivekananda is unequivocally endorsing the *Advaita Vedanta* view of the oneness of *Atman* and Divinity. The real man transcends time, space, and causation and is free. The apparent man, bound by time, space, and causation, is bonded and is not free. *Vedanta* concludes that *Moksha* (liberation from this bondage) is the purpose of life.

Swami Vivekananda reinforces that true happiness cannot be found in anything that is evanescent, like the senses. True happiness is in yourself, the infinite spirit. Swami Vivekananda highlights that the ignorance of the real man and the apparent man is the greatest misery. Just like Adi Shankaracharya propounded that *Maya* (ignorance) was the key reason for not attaining spiritual liberation,.

Swami concludes by advising us to have a relentless pursuit to realize the ultimate truth, which is the Real Man in all of us.

"The goal may be distant, but awake, arise, and stop not till the goal is reached."

Can the infinite become the finite?

The concept of Advaita Vedanta, which we discussed before, can be expressed as the visual below to satisfy the needs of Western philosophers and scientists.

Advaita explained

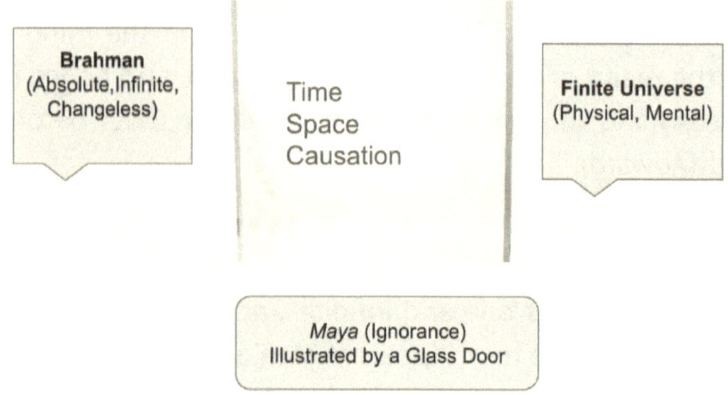

Advaita Vedanta, which Swami Vivekananda re-enforces, is characterized by an infinite entity, *Brahman*, that can only be realized by transcending the mind, and hence time, space, and causation. The power of *Maya* (ignorance) is the lens or glass through which the finite universe is experienced. Unveiling this maya leads us to realize the infinite absolute. While this theory seems to explain universality, inquisitive-minded Western philosophers and scientists want an answer to the question, "How has the infinite, the absolute, become the finite?"?

Various *Advaita* philosophers have used *Maya* as the unveiling power of Brahman (as we discussed in previous chapters) to explain the cause of superimposition or error (*Adhyasa*), thus explaining the plurality of the appearance of the universe. Swami Vivekananda uses the same examples of waves in the ocean being different names (*nama*) and forms (*rupa*) of the water to explain plurality, and the wave has no existence without the underlying substratum, which is the ocean.

To answer the Western philosophical minds who question the superimposition theory, Swami Vivekananda has a blunter answer. He says that there is no answer to the above question and points out the contradictory nature of the question. If this question were answered, there would be no absolute; it has become finite. He says the absolute can never be known, as knowing involves objectification and involves the mind stuff. Oneness in Advaita cannot be objectified.

To the academics or the analytical minds, the above might be a bit disheartening that the Advaita philosophy cannot be explained as clearly as a mathematical proof or scientifically proven. Swami does not want spiritual seekers to have a defeatist attitude, that God is unknowable, and hence why bother? He says, quoting the *Vedas,* "God is neither known nor unknown, but something infinitely higher than either. He is your self."

Swami also answers the dualists (*Dvaita* and *Visishtadvaita* schools) who criticize Advaita for still proposing a dual reality, *Brahman* and *Maya,* and hence invalidating the oneness theory of *Advaita.* For duality to hold true, there must be two absolute independent existences, and *Maya,* which is time, space, and causation, CANNOT be independent. He proves that time, space, and causation cannot have independent existence, and hence, in reality, there is only one reality, Brahman. He compares *Maya* to a shadow that you cannot catch and has no real existence, but you cannot deny that it does not exist. So, shadows neither exist nor do not exist, just like *Maya.* Only by transcending time, space, and causality, going beyond senses and the mind, can *Maya* disappear, unveiling the ever-existent, infinite, Absolute (*Brahman*).

Swami also answers why renunciation (Vairagya) is underscored in *Vedanta,* including the *Bhagavad Gita.* The cynic or materialist may shrug this off as evading responsibilities or 'giving up', while in reality it means just the opposite. Renunciation is moving away from this world the way we see it, filled with *Maya* and our creation, due to ignorance. When we renounce this world, the only thing that remains is God. Swami instructs us to see God in everyone and everything, a beautiful appeal of universality that made Swami Vivekananda's teachings so inclusive and secular. This is akin to the sun rising, where once the darkness of night is unveiled, the only thing that remains is light, and everything is light.

THE INTERNAL MAN AND IMMORTALITY OF *ATMAN*

Swami Vivekananda explains the Vedantic concept of the soul (Atman) in terms of being self-luminous. He propounds that the body and mind are just matter, and dull and evanescent matter cannot be knowledge or self-luminous. Only the Atman (soul) can make this dull matter self-luminous. One example he discusses is the perspective of vision and hearing. In both cases, information transfer happens from the sense organs to the brain's nerve center, to the mind, to the intellect, and eventually to the soul (Atman), and in the reverse direction for actions produced from the senses.

He then distinguishes the subtle difference between the essence and qualities of the atman. Qualities are borrowed and hence evanescent; essence is permanent and self-luminous. Atman does **not** have the qualities of knowledge, existence, and bliss, but instead they **are** the essence of the soul.

He further extends this theory that a self-luminous, independent soul could not have been created. It always existed, and there was never a time when it never existed, as it could not have been the outcome of anything. It transcends time, space, and causation, and hence is the Absolute, the infinite.

Swami logically deduces the equality of the Atman and Brahman.

Since Atman is the only existence in the human body that is immaterial (body and mind are material), it cannot thus be a compound (matter) and hence does not follow the law of cause and effect, and so it is immortal. That which is immortal can have no beginning, since everything that has a beginning must have an end. Atman is formless since anything with form is subject to force and matter. Since it is formless, it is not conditioned in space and hence is omniscient or ever-pervading. Thus, it is proven that Atman (the self) transcends time (omnipresent), space (omniscient), and causation (immortal), and hence is the absolute reality, or Brahman. It is hence immortal, concludes Swami, re-emphasizing a truth of enormous significance that was discussed in the *Upanishads*.

Duality

Swami Vivekananda strongly argued that monistic philosophy, or *Advaita Vedanta,* is the only true reality. He says, quoting the *Bhagavad Gita,* "In this world of many, he who sees the One, in the ever-changing world, he who sees Him who never changes, as the soul of his own soul, as his own self, he is free, he is blessed, he has reached the goal." He then reiterates the *Advaita Mahavakya "Tat Tvam Asi"* (You Are That), signifying the unity between *Atman* and *Brahman,* as Adi Shankaracharya propounded.

He had issues with duality that made a man weaker by indoctrinating another power as the controller, creator, and destroyer of human destiny. Swami strongly believed that duality created divisions and led to misrepresentations of how to achieve liberation. He did not have any issues with the concept of personal God (*Saguna Brahman*) as long as there was a realization that the ultimate reality of Brahman is one without a second. He strongly believed that more than 90% of the world is dualistic (religion of the masses), as human nature finds it hard to grasp anything beyond the intellect. Monism (*Advaita*) is especially harder to comprehend due to the abstract and absolute oneness theories of the monists. Swami questions the thought beyond all-powerful personal GODS who can only have good attributes and no evil. He logically argues that good and evil are two sides of the same coin, and one cannot exist without the other. The same way light cannot exist without darkness or life cannot exist without death.

He postulated that whenever there is duality (more than one), there is delusion, danger, fear, conflict, and strife. When only ONE exists and divinity is within the soul, there is no one to hate, no one to struggle with, no one to fight with.

Advaita

Swami Vivekananda was a staunch *Advaitin*, and he laments that in India, the birthplace of Vedanta and Advaita Vedanta, very few people have been able to understand this philosophy. He points to the weakness in man—to lean on something higher—that is not his self (dualistic), sort of a "comfortable religion" that impedes the masses from truly understanding and practicing Advaita Vedanta. The whole of this universe is one unity, one existence. He echoes the Advaita Vedanta core philosophy that for each one of us, the apparent duality or diversity is *Brahman* plus *Maya*. If we get rid of this *Maya* (ignorance), each one of us will unveil what we truly are, *Brahman*.

PART III

CONTEMPORARY WESTERN AND SCIENTIFIC PHILOSOPHY

CHAPTER 13

PURPOSE FIRST, PROCESS NEXT

PURPOSE

From the entirety of Vedanta and the modern interpretation of Neo Vedanta, the purpose of human life is *Moksha* (liberation). *Moksha* is the ultimate spiritual goal, and the goal is to be *free* and achieve eternal bliss.

Freedom from what, you might ask?

Freedom from ignorance, fear, suffering, discontentment, anger, jealousy, material attachments, momentary happiness, bondage with the material world—everything we think is part of living.

Vedanta unequivocally claims that our souls are divine, and it is a pity that we cannot find the true greatness that lies within us. The purpose of everyone's life should be to discover their true selves.

If you find the above purpose highly ideological, I don't blame you! The ancient sages who relayed the message of God as *Vedas* realized that freedom is the ultimate virtue of man, as the soul (which is the real self) is eternally free. They saw human suffering and described an elaborate way (as we have discussed in the first two parts) of how to achieve ultimate freedom, eternal bliss, and oneness with the universe.

Vedanta's key subject is 'You the self'; no one else. There is an overarching message that can be ascertained by simplifying the ideological teachings of Vedanta. The entire human race and all living beings in the universe, both immanent and transcendent, are undoubtedly conditioned by two key motives or purposes in life.

- *Sukha Prapti* (Yearning for Joy)

- *Duhkha Nivrtti* (revulsion from sorrow)

We may manage joy or avoid sorrow for some time, but it's always fleeting, ever-alluding, and never-enduring.

If we achieve to obtain enduring levels of happiness, peace, and tranquility, we are 'enlightened' or free (*Jivan Mukta*). In this enlightened state, the individual has gained mastery of body, mind, and intellect and is always in a state of inner peace and joy, unfettered by the ever-changing, turbulent world surrounding him.

Some Western philosophers accuse Vedanta of being self-centered due to its focus on the individual self. These claims could not be any farther than the truth. The truth is, that the enlightened person is full of love and compassion for everyone around him, and one such enlightened person inspires an entire generation to seek freedom and liberation. The Vedanta culture is laden with such enlightened minds who are shining beacons of Eastern philosophy, one that continues to thrive and expand through thousands of years and will continue forever!

Being enlightened does not mean being a stone or a stoic. There may be instances where the enlightened person may be perceived as 'indifferent' or 'unemotional' by mere mortals. The enlightened person does indeed experience emotions, but he does not let them overpower him. "Such a person has an emotion, but he does not **become** the emotion," says Swami Chinmayananda. The Bhagavad Gita also emphasizes the behavior of an emotional person in this rather paradoxical statement that, when deeply analyzed, reveals the truth.

कर्मण्यकर्म यः पश्येद् अकर्मणि च कर्म यः।

स बुद्धिमान् मनुष्येषु स युक्तः कृत्स्नकर्मकृत्।।4.18।।

Karmanya karma yaḥ paśyed Akarmaṇi ca karma yaḥ Sa buddhimān manuṣyeṣu Sa yuktaḥ kṛtsna-karma-kṛt

"One who sees inaction in action and action in inaction is intelligent among men, and he is in the transcendental position, although engaged in all kinds of work."

The enlightened person (*yogi*) is always engaged in action but never strives to be attached to the results of the actions. This verse underscores that the process is more important than just the goal. The journey is more important than the destination.

The second part of the verse underscores that what others perceive as inaction is deeply actionable for the enlightened person. This includes being completely conscious and having a sense of heightened awareness all the time. This is also termed mindfulness by Western philosophers and will be discussed in the later chapters.

Swami Vivekananda eloquently summarized, "Each soul is potentially divine, and the goal is to manifest divinity by controlling nature, both external and internal. Do this either by work, or worship, or psychic control, or philosophy—by one, or more, or all of these—and be free.".

In this diligent and tireless journey toward spiritual liberation, happiness, peace, and joy happen to be "side effects." Well, who doesn't want that? Paradoxically, we have been told to "pursue happiness," but in reality, Vedanta claims happiness and contentment happen to be along the way toward achieving eternal bliss and unity with the divine. We must make this switch toward not just pursuing happiness as a single-minded object but striving for a higher purpose. That is the single most important truth that Vedanta hits you with!!!

In the book Authentic Happiness, famed psychologist Martin Seligman uses the following quotes from contemporary psychologists: Modern Western philosophers support this claim that we cannot reach happiness by consciously searching for it. Famous Western philosopher J.S. Mill says, "Ask yourself whether you are happy, and you cease to be so." Another famous Austrian psychologist summarizes, "Don't aim at success (happiness)—the more you aim at it and make it a target, the more it must ensue... as the unintended side-effect of one's personal dedication to a course greater than oneself."

Vedanta unequivocally declares that Atman (individual self) is beyond body, mind, and intellect. Happiness is a state of mind and, hence, is transient. The goal is to transcend the body, mind, and intellect through the four types of yoga described in the previous chapters. Only then is there a glimpse of eternal bliss.

Have I reached a state of eternal bliss? Absolutely not. But every day of living is getting me closer, and I strive to continue till I get there!

"Arise, awaken, and stop not until the goal is reached."

Your mind is stronger than your body.

Your intellect is stronger than your mind.

Your will is stronger than your intellect.

You (the eternal *Atman*) are stronger than your will.

Are you ready to come on this journey with me?

Process – Methods for freedom

Armed with the strong purpose that we discussed in the previous section, we now explore the process that one can engage in to reach the ultimate reality and strive toward the ultimate bliss.

The true purpose of the Vedantic scriptures, including the *Bhagavad Gita,* is to elucidate methods to achieve this freedom. At a very high-level, the Vedantic scriptures clearly illuminate the four paths of yoga toward spiritual liberation and what I call the "2-fold I-path."

- I-lessness: Transcending the impermanent body and mind stuff.

- Inner focus: Attention Inward rather than outward

The above may be a gross oversimplification of the many facets of the Vedantic scriptures, but it's essential to simplify this to make it meaningful in our complex everyday lives.

It always helps to visualize the two-fold **I-path** to constantly reinforce these paths of liberation.

Chapter 14

I-LESSNESS

Melting the sense of **I**, the same way a candle melts to give us light. What is left at the end is pure light that dispels ignorance (*Avidya*) and reveals knowledge (*Jnana*). A famous mantra from the Brihadaranyaka Upanishad illustrates the point.

"Asatoma Jyotirgamaya"

Asatoma: Lead from the unreal (illusion) to the real (truth).

Jyotirgamaya: Lead me from darkness to light.

Why is it so important to strive for I-lessness? The I that we, as humans, use ONLY describes transient states. Our body changes, our mind changes, our intellect changes, and our thoughts and emotions change. We have to strive to 'maintain a distance' between the true I (Atman), which is permanent, unchanging, and imperishable, and, according to Advaita, one with Brahman (ultimate reality).

While it is almost impossible for most humans to completely lose the transient nature of I, it behooves us to try to get there with deep spiritual practice through the four types of yoga.

Ramana Maharshi, a Hindu sage and liberated soul (*Jivan Mukta*), explained the concept of I beautifully.

According to Ramana Maharshi, the I-thought is the sense of individuality; "I am this" or "I am that" is the ego. By paying attention to the 'I'-thought and inquiring where it comes from, the 'I'-thought will disappear, and the shining forth of self-awareness will appear. This results in an effortless awareness of being, and by staying with it, this "gradually destroys the *vasanas* (mind impressions) that cause the 'I'-thought to rise". When the *vasanas* (mind impression) disappear, the mind, *vritti*, also comes to rest since it centers around the 'I'-thought, and finally the 'I'-thought never rises again, which is self-realization or liberation.

Chapter 15

INNER FOCUS

The visual that often helps me sharpen my inner focus is comparing the turbulent surface of the ocean (akin to an external world with sensory distractions) to the serene deep ocean, which personifies tranquility and stillness analogs to an ideal state of mind to achieve spiritual liberation.

Our daily lives are like the choppy surface of the ocean, with huge waves created by outward and external sensory-based interactions. We are always in the 'reactionary' mode. Mental restlessness results from an outward focus of our awareness. True happiness can never be found outside of self. No amount of material possessions or wealth can make you enduringly happy.

"Possessions of material riches without inner peace are like dying of thirst while bathing in a lake," says Paramahamsa Yogananda.

Sensory happiness is only temporal in nature and can be termed "pleasure", while 'inner' happiness is termed "joy," "peace," and "Awareness". They are starkly different, and a conscious effort is needed to realize the latter.

Chapter 16

LEVELS OF HAPPINESS

According to the ancient and profound Greek philosopher Aristotle, there are four levels of happiness.

This is illustrated in the visual below.

The lowest form of happiness is also the most temporal and is short-lived. This is the happiness derived from external material objects and sensual pleasures. Most of us spend our entire life span at this lower level of happiness, clamoring for a bigger house, a better car, a better job, and a higher salary. There is no end to the desires of the human mind.

Levels of Happiness

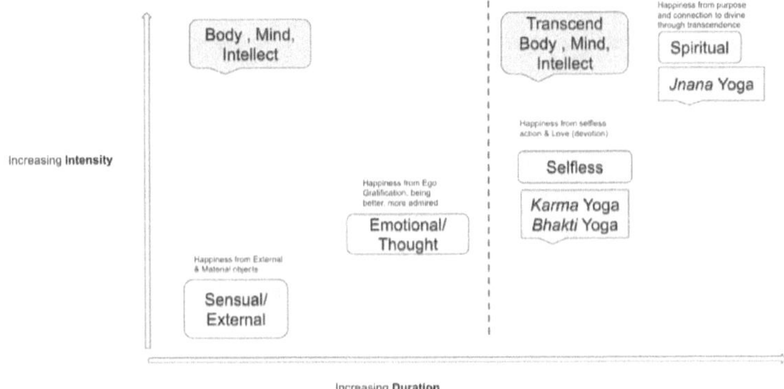

Swami Chinmayananda (a famous theologian and founder of the Chinmaya mission) proposes a very simple formula for happiness in the form of a mathematical equation.

Happiness =

So, in essence, happiness can be increased by decreasing the denominator by having fewer desires, and that's the key essence of the term *vairagya* (renunciation or detachment from worldly desires and possessions) used in the Upanishads and the Bhagavad Gita. Happiness can also be increased by increasing the numerator, increasing the number of desires fulfilled. We know that desires have no end, and expecting otherwise is analogous to dropping a stone in still water and expecting no ripples.

Swami Vivekananda eloquently commented that "if the power to satisfy our desires increased in arithmetic progression, the power of desire increased in geometric progression."

There is another famous quote (which we have discussed previously) from the *Bhagavad Gita* that explains this vicious circle. The Supreme Lord (*Saguna Brahman*) Krishna advises the following on desires:.

"While contemplating the objects of the senses, a person develops attachment for them, and from such attachment, lust develops, and from lust, anger arises."

"From anger, complete delusion arises, and from delusion, bewilderment of memory. When memory is bewildered, intelligence is lost, and when intelligence is lost, one falls down again into the material pool."

"But a person free from all attachment and aversion and able to control his senses through regulative principles of freedom can obtain the complete mercy of the Lord."

These verses highlight the futility of the progression of sensual attachment and desires.

The second level of happiness is a bit more enduring than pure sensual pleasures but still involves the human ego. In this 'emotional' happiness, there is a clamoring for admiration and winning beyond all costs. While this level of happiness may be a bit more enduring, it eventually leads to self-absorption, jealousy, cynicism, and oppression of others. The first two levels of happiness involve the body, mind, and ego.

The third and fourth levels of happiness get into the Vedantic solution of yoga, implying moving beyond (transcending) the self (body, mind, and intellect). The third ladder of happiness can be compared to the selfless action of work (Karma Yoga) and selfless devotion and love. This selfless devotion and love can be for any cause greater than yourself, whether it be saving the planet, saving the animals, feeding the impoverished, or random acts of kindness. The happiness from these selfless acts lasts longer and is scientifically proven to do so. When this love and devotion are for the supreme Lord (*Saguna Brahman)*, then it becomes *Bhakti Yoga*.

You may have witnessed the enduring levels of happiness when you impart kindness to random strangers. Say letting someone take your parking spot or letting someone board earlier than you on a flight, or helping a random person with their heavy luggage with no expectation in return.

Working for a cause or a charity organization is another great example of enduring happiness, as long as there is no motive that traces itself back to you. Unfortunately, most charity organizations these days have more glamour and less substance.

The highest level of enduring happiness is the one found in a life with a purpose larger than yourself or the universe. One that transcends our changing body, mind, and intellect. In monotheistic religions, it is the enduring yearning to reach the abode of God (Saguna Brahman), and in monistic religion (Advaita), it is realizing the divinity of your soul (*Atman*) and the unity of *Atman* and *Brahman* (ultimate reality). We have discussed the four paths of yoga in previous chapters to achieve the ultimate reality (Brahman).

The state of happiness achieved in the process of the spiritual journey is said to be eternally peaceful and infinitely blissful and is termed enlightenment. All the world's major religions preach to mankind to strive to achieve this stage. We have discussed the various names that Vedanta attributes to this state.

- *Sat-Chit-Ananda* (Existence-Consciousness-Bliss)
- *Moksha* (Liberation)
- *Samadhi* (the highest state of bliss)
- *Nirvana* (a common Buddhist term also found in Vedanta)

- *Sat-Chit-Ananda* (Existence-Consciousness-Bliss)
- *Moksha* (Liberation)
- *Samadhi* (the highest state of bliss)
- *Nirvana* (a common Buddhist term also found in Vedanta)

Chapter 17

HAPPINESS AS DEFINED BY MODERN PSYCHOLOGISTS

It is imperative to note that the Vedantic view of eternal bliss or enduring happiness is very 'subjective' and one needs to 'experience' it for oneself. It cannot be objectively measured, as it's beyond the scope of the human mind and intellect.

"The Supreme State is not accessible to the understanding of the common man. One can only understand It by becoming It." Says Swami Vivekananda.

However, this has not deterred several psychologists in the West from 'objectively' defining enduring happiness. One such attempt at an objective definition was made in the world of positive psychology by renowned psychologist Martin Seligman. He says, "Positive psychology takes you through the countryside of pleasure and gratification, up into the high country of strength and virtue, and finally to the peaks of lasting fulfillment, meaning, and purpose." Dr. Seligman is re-iterating the ladders of happiness from the viewpoint of positive psychology.

Seligman comes up with his own definition of an enduring level of happiness:

$$H = S + C + V$$

H is the individual's 'enduring' level of happiness.

S is the individual set range, which, according to Seligman, is genetic (you would be happy if your parents were) and relies on our adaptability to good things and taking them for granted, which leads to an asymptote in happiness level (this is termed the hedonic treadmill). A classic example is the first bite of your favorite dessert or food, and with every bite comes an exponentially decaying sense of happiness, which we eventually adapt to.

C is the Circumstances of your life that have a bearing on your enduring happiness include things like how much money you have, how social you are, whether you are married, whether you live in a safe and prosperous country, and how healthy you are, among other things.

V is the factor under your (voluntary) control and is primarily the subject of his book.

In developing a theory to address this, Seligman selected five components that people pursue and are under their voluntary control (V) because they are intrinsically motivating and contribute to wellbeing. These elements are defined and measured independently of each other. He came up with the PERMA model, which attempts to'measure' happiness or state of wellbeing.

The PERMA model has five components.

- ♦ P: Positive Emotion
- ♦ E: Engagement
- ♦ R: Relationships
- ♦ M -Meaning
- ♦ A: Accomplishments

In the ladders of happiness we discussed earlier, these five attributes can be distributed as illustrated in the visual below.

Levels of Happiness

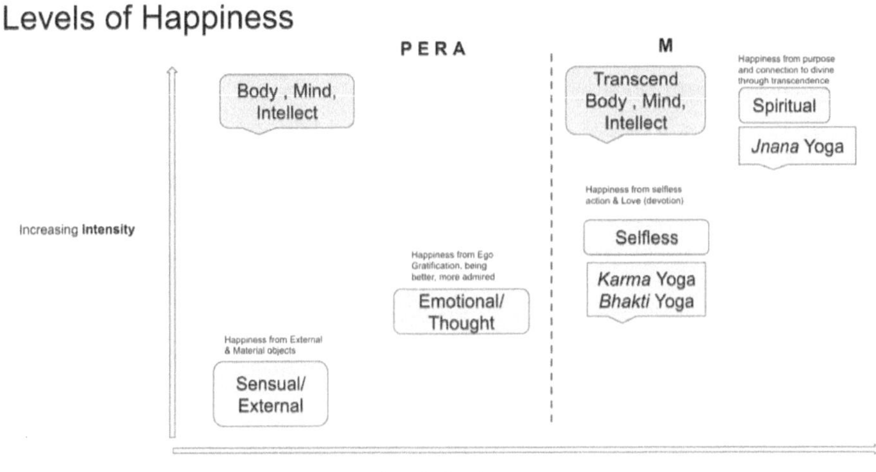

Let's delve a bit deeper into each of the five attributes outlined by Dr. Seligman.

P: Positive Emotions

Dr. Seligman identifies positive emotions into three kinds.

Positive emotions (from the past): these include satisfaction, contentment, pride, and serenity.

Positive emotions (into the future): these include optimism, hope, confidence, trust, and faith.

It is important to note that the positive emotions about the past and future are still felt in the 'present'. You cannot time-travel!

At any moment, it is possible to 'feel' emotions (positive or negative) about the past and the future. Positive psychologists, including Seligman, highlight the importance of focusing on positive emotions in the present to increase your enduring happiness (H). You cannot change the past, you cannot see the future, and the only thing relevant is the present. This by no way implies you have erased your past or are less optimistic about the future; it only means you can increase your enduring happiness (H) by focusing your energy where you can actually affect the outcome, which is the present, and not worrying about the past or the future.

This chapter focuses more on the positive emotions in the *present*.

According to Seligman, Positive emotions are divided into two types: pleasures and gratifications.

Pleasures are further classified into:

lower pleasures, like bodily pleasures

higher pleasures such as thrills, euphoria, and excitement

The lower pleasures are immediate, come through the senses, and are momentary. This is the lowest level on the happiness scale, yet most of mankind mostly clings to this level.

The higher pleasures are a bit more cognitive and tend to last a bit longer, but they are still not enduring and are still considered the lowest level on the happiness scale. An example is when you feel excited to watch a game, attend a concert, get euphoric when you meet your favorite celebrity, or feel the thrill of an amusement park ride. These are just a few examples, and all of them end quickly and do not have enduring levels of happiness.

We have discussed in the previous sections that it is futile to maximize the 'quantity' of these lower and higher pleasures, but Dr. Seligman proposes techniques to increase the 'quality' of these pleasures.

He proposes a few techniques that one can find valuable in everyday life to enhance the quantity of our pleasurable experiences.

1. **Self-restraint** by spreading the pleasurable events out in time and reducing repeat indulgence in the same pleasure.

   Self-restraint is discussed heavily in Vedanta as a foundational characteristic for spiritual liberation and was discussed in earlier chapters. It is the practice of controlling one's external senses and desires. It involves consciously managing and moderating sensory inputs and cravings to prevent them from overwhelming the mind and leading to impulsive or harmful actions

2. Making it pleasurable for others through random and surprise **acts of kindness** Calling an old friend, helping a random stranger with something meaningful, a thoughtful gift, or a note for someone are some examples.

3. **Mindfulness** is the technique of focusing the mind's full attention in the present moment (now) without any judgment or distraction. It is a complete state of awareness of the present. Western society has embraced mindfulness, which is often used synonymously with stress reduction and emotional wellbeing. Typically, mindfulness is practiced through diligent meditation, where the focus is to bring awareness from external to internal by paying attention to one's breath, among other things. Recently, mindfulness studies have emerged to expand mindfulness to eating, walking, having conversations, or just about anything in the conscious life. I will discuss a proven meditation technique that has worked for me to be fully conscious most of the time.

Mindfulness is a rather new philosophical practice among Western psychologists and is heavily influenced by Hinduism and Buddhist techniques. It is a tiny subset of the self-awareness and self-realization techniques highlighted in the teachings of Vedanta. Mindfulness has a lower goal: enhancing the quantity of pleasures for stress reduction, while Vedantic techniques have a higher goal: reaching the most enduring level of happiness and union with the absolute.

The word mindful itself is a bit paradoxical, where in actuality the goal is to empty the mind of past impressions and future speculations, making room for savoring the present and only the present. In the bestselling book "Power of Now," Eckart Tolle, a contemporary spiritual teacher, highlights that the only important time is the one we think about the least: the present. The reason only the present matters is that everything *happens* here. Everything you feel and sense takes place in the present. He then elucidates that "the past is nothing more than all present moments that have gone by, and the future is just a collection of present moments waiting to arrive."

Dr Seligman defines a term called 'pleasant life' which is "life that successfully pursues the positive emotions about the present, past and future".

This book does **not** cover the positive emotions about the past and future and the reader can find more details in the book Authentic Happiness by Dr Seligman. The visual below highlights the three forms of positive emotions.

Increasing Positive Emotions

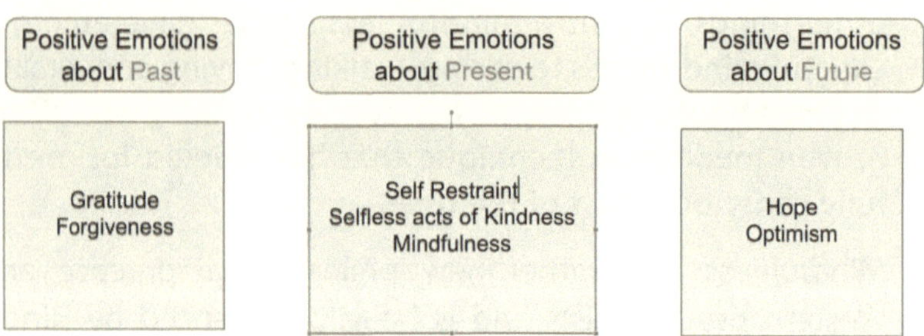

E-ENGAGEMENT

Next up on the happiness ladder is Engagement and according to Dr. Seligman, engagement leads to gratification. He distinguishes between pleasures and gratifications, which, at a cursory glance, might mean the same to an impetuous reader. He defines gratification as positive emotions about the present, and unlike pleasures, they are NOT feelings but activities we like doing: reading, rock climbing, coding, hiking, dancing, having a good conversation with others, and being very personal to the individual.

He defines this state of engagement as "Total absorption" "Suspension of Consciousness" "Complete absence of Emotions". Note that the term 'Consciousness' used by Western psychologists like Dr. Seligman still involves the mind stuff and is starkly different from Vedanta, where consciousness (*chit*) or awareness transcends the mind.

However, it is key to note that engagement, as described by Dr. Seligman, involves going beyond the mind and moving beyond emotions, and that's similar to what we have been discussing previously in terms of the essence of the Vedantic teachings. Here, you find the first implicit endorsement of the Vedantic teachings from modern psychology to achieve enduring happiness. Many Western scholars and psychologists are still oblivious to the fact that Vedanta is more comprehensive and has been preaching this philosophy of eternal joy or enduring happiness for thousands of years!!

The gratifications acquired due to engagement in activities enable you to lose yourself and be completely absorbed, losing track of time. When one loses track of time, he transcends the mind; the concept of time is hidden deep in our minds. Mind-lessness is the same as time-lessness. The concept of complete absorption is called FLOW and was developed by renowned psychologist Dr. Mihaly Csikszentmihalyi and elucidated in his bestselling book "FLOW." We will discuss key aspects of this book in the next section.

WHAT IS FLOW?

While this concept was independently researched by psychologist Dr. Mihaly in modern times, the great Indian sage Patanjali explained this concept called *Dharana* (which we covered in the earlier chapters) as one of the eight limbs (*Ashtanga*) toward spiritual enlightenment. Here are some verses from the Yoga Sutras of Patanjali that illustrate the concept of *Dharana* (flow or concentration).

1. "Dharana is the binding of the mind to one place, object, or idea."

   ♦ Yoga Sutras 3.1

2. "One-pointedness of mind is dharana."

   ♦ Yoga Sutras 3.1

3. "When the mind has been trained to remain fixed on a certain internal or external location, there comes to it the power of flowing in an unbroken current."

   ♦ Yoga Sutras 3.9

4. "The process of achieving one-pointedness is like the **flow** of oil from one vessel to another."

   ♦ Yoga Sutras 3.41

5. "By the one-pointedness of this discipline, the radiance that is inherent in the object of meditation shines forth."

   ♦   Yoga Sutras 3.45

Dr. Mihaly's book explains this gratification achieved through FLOW to the modern reader with certain examples, which all of us can relate to in our mundane lives.

"Playing a close game of tennis that stretches one's ability is enjoyable, as is reading a book that reveals things in a new light, as is having a conversation that leads us to express ideas we didn't know we had. Closing a contested business deal, or any piece of work well done, is enjoyable. None of these experiences may have been particularly pleasurable at the time, but afterward, we think back on them and say, 'That was fun' and wish they would happen again."

All the above examples are **not** pleasures but gratifications that last longer and have a noble purpose.

The components involved in various gratifications experienced when we are in FLOW are notably similar. They are,

   ♦   The task is challenging and requires skill.

   ♦   We concentrate.

   ♦   There are clear goals.

   ♦   We get immediate feedback.

   ♦   We have deep, effortless involvement.

   ♦   There is a sense of control.

   ♦   Our sense of self vanishes.

   ♦   Time stops.

It is very clear from the above that there are no positive emotions like pleasures listed, as the key is the 'absence' of emotions or moving beyond the mind or moving beyond the self that leads to gratifications and inch us ever closer to eternal joy. This is one of the examples of the I-lessness we discussed in the two-fold I-path in the earlier sections.

A visual depicting activity that can generate flow is shown on the next page. Dr. Mihaly stresses that the activities we engage in should have a fine balance between skill and challenge, and there should be a continuous evolution toward the top. Activity that requires high amounts of skill but requires no challenge leads to boredom and will not create a state of flow. As an example, a high schooler solves kindergarten math problems. A top tennis player is a novice! On the contrary, activities that are highly challenging and in which you possess little to no skills create anxiety and will not generate flow. As an example, a junior player playing Novak Djokovic in a game of tennis or an amateur playing chess with the grandmaster!

For optimal flow, the skill and challenge need to be fairly balanced, and the challenges need to increase as skills develop. The continuous evolution of this creates a flow state.

It is clear from the carefully detailed scientific studies that choosing gratification over pleasure is the right choice, so given a choice between watching sitcoms on TV or curling up with a good book, our decision will have an impact on enduring happiness or momentary pleasure.

Dr. Seligman offers powerful advice to choose gratification over pleasures: gratification through total engagement results in a flow and leads to the absence of feeling and loss of self-consciousness, while pleasures are all about "self-absorption," leading to narcissism and depression. The pleasures come easily, and the gratifications require skill and effort, and exercising one's personal strengths and virtues is obviously hard.

FLOW FOR EVER

Turning your entire life into a unified flow experience.

Is there such a thing? Dr. Mihaly unequivocally says it is absolutely plausible. He says, "If a person sets out to achieve a difficult enough goal, from which all other goals logically follow," then it is possible to give 'meaning' to one's life. It's the 'meaningful' life that's full of flow, per Dr. Mihaly.

Optimal FLOW state

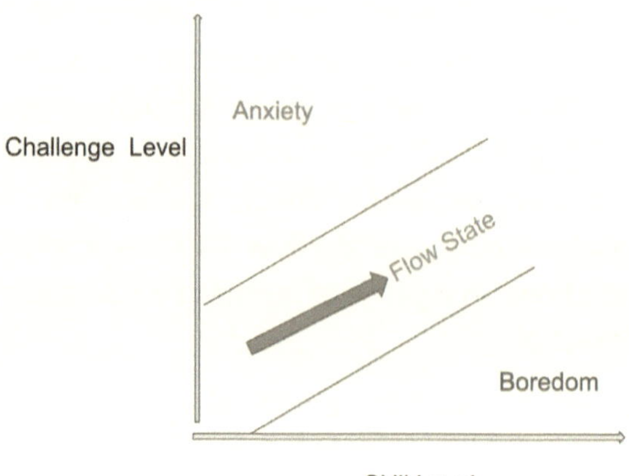

Dr Mihaly does not bring any religious references into this higher goal, while Dr Seligman does when he discusses the M (meaning) in this PERMA model. It is rather harmonious that the two leading researchers concur on the highest ladder of enduring happiness.

We have learned from Vedanta that the highest goal from which all the goals follow is the goal of *Moksha,* or liberation, or self-realization, or God-realization.

If one were to be consciously engaged in the quest for this eternal bliss, even science-based social psychologists agree that the entirety of life can be an experience of FLOW and is not just limited to activities of Engagement.

Dr Mihaly elucidates three ways to achieve this 'meaningful' life.

1. Purpose: A goal challenging enough to take up all the energies.

2. Resolution: action toward achieving this challenging goal.

3. Harmony between purpose and resolution.

There is amazing consonance when we draw parallels to the four paths of yoga that Vedanta prescribes to the modern social psychologist's view of enduring happiness or eternal bliss.

Purpose is the path of Jnana Yoga to realize the true nature of *Brahman* as Atman per monistic view or the supreme abode (*Saguna Brahman*) in monotheistic view. This *Jnana* (knowledge) of realizing or reaching the omniscient, omnipresent Brahman is the real 'purpose' of Vedanta.

'Resolution' of the above purpose comes in the form of karma yoga (selfless actions). Bhakti Yoga (selfless devotion or self) or Raja Yoga (dissolving the sense of I in the superconscious state of *samadhi*)

'Harmony' is what brings the seamless blending of the four paths of yoga into our daily lives.

Science-based social psychologists attribute the universe in which we live and the individuality we have to the "differentiation" of the mind. However, they all agree that the"integration"of the mind, wherein we feel one with this universe, is the underdeveloped component of the mind and is the task of the next decades and centuries. Little did they realize that this "integration of the mind," which is unity with the universe, was proclaimed by *Vedanta* thousands of years ago! We are blessed to have the faculty to absorb these gems of wisdom.

Strength and virtue as foundations of gratitude

Dr. Seligman digs further and argues that engagement CANNOT be obtained by bodily pleasures, nor can it be chemically induced or attained by any shortcuts. It can only be achieved by enacting personal strengths and virtues.

Dr. Seligman defines six core virtues that he and his team of researchers believed were rooted in every major religion of the world, from the *Upanishads* to the Koran, the Old Testament of Christianity, Buddha, Aristotle, and Plato, among others. They are,

1. Wisdom and knowledge

2. Courage

3. Love and humanity

4. Justice

5. Temperance

6. Spirituality and transcendence

Due to the abstract nature of these virtues that define the 'character' of the individual, Dr. Seligman and his team of researchers came up with twenty-four strengths that are 'means' to achieving these six virtues.

Dr. Seligman has a website, www.authetichappiness.org for readers to take the strength survey. I did the survey to identify my top five 'signature' strengths that define the authentic self. I highly recommend readers take this survey.

The twenty-four strengths that Dr. Seligman discusses are detailed below. This book will not delve into the details of these strengths because they are reasonably self-explanatory.

Virtue 1: Wisdom and Knowledge

1. Curiosity and interest in the world

2. Love of learning

3. Judgment/Critical thinking/open-mindedness

4. Ingenuity, Originality, Practical Intelligence, and Street Smarts

5. Social intelligence, personal intelligence, and emotional intelligence

6. Perspective

Virtue 2: Courage

1. Valor and bravery

2. Perseverance/Industry/Diligence

3. Integrity/Genuineness/Honesty

Virtue 3: Humanity and Love

1. Kindness and generosity

2. Loving and allowing oneself to be loved

Virtue 4: Justice

1. Citizenship/Duty/Teamwork/Loyalty

   2. Fairness and equity

   3. Leadership

Virtue 5: Temperance

   1. Self-control

   2. Prudence/Discretion/Caution

   3. Humility and modesty

Virtue 6: Transcendence

   1. Appreciation of beauty and excellence

   2. Gratitude

   3. Hope/Optimism/Future-Mindedness

   4. Spirituality/Sense of Purpose/Faith/Religiousness

   5. Forgiveness and mercy

   6. Playfulness and humor

   7. Zest/Passion/Enthusiasm

Dr. Seligman advises us to identify our top five strengths and use them abundantly in our relationships (at work, family, parenting, etc.). That becomes the R in the PERMA model.

He then defines a higher form of life, the 'good life', which is higher than the 'pleasant life', as "using signature strengths every day in the main realms of life to bring abundant gratification and authentic happiness."

Dr. Seligman finally wraps up with a discussion of a meaningful life, which is the M in the PERMA model. He says, "A meaningful life is the one that joins with something larger than who we are, and the larger the something is, the more meaning our lives have." He then tersely defines the 'meaningful' life as using your signature strengths and virtues in the service of something much larger than you.

Akin to most Western psychologists, Dr. Seligman does not get into the details of the M in the PERMA mode. That hard problem of meaning has already been solved by our great sages and *rishis* by singing the voice of God as part of the *Vedas* and the *Upanishads*.

Vedanta not only validates most of the PERMA concepts but goes significantly beyond. According to Vedanta, meaningful life is the realization of Brahman, the ultimate reality, the largest of them all!

PART IV

PERSONAL & PRACTICAL INSIGHTS

Chapter 18

INTRODUCTION

This is the last and concluding part of our book, and I feel like a recap of what we have discussed is in order.

Part I discussed the Vedas, Upanishads, and the Bhagavad Gita, along with major schools of Hinduism.

Part II discussed the Neo Vedanta, which included a fusion of the knowledge of Vedanta sprinkled with Western philosophy.

Part III discussed contemporary Western social psychologists' views on enduring happiness and the correlation with Vedantic teachings.

Part IV will discuss the personal insights and guidelines based on my 'subjective' and 'experiential' application of the teachings in daily life.

The goal of this book is to open the window of my personal insights into this quest for enduring joy, or self-realization, or as modern Western social psychologists refer to it, 'wellbeing'. This quest has turned into a discovery of a higher purpose and filled my life with meaning that eluded me for four and a half decades of my life.

I have spent the last few years taking an analytical approach to this and imbibing from the source, the *Vedas* and the *Upanishads*. I have to admit that this has mostly been *Svadhyaya* (self-study) splintered with inspirations from these great souls in the form of books. The serendipity with *Svadhyaya* is a lack of objective tainting of a particular subject matter. There are too many opinions in this world from lots of preachers. It's you and the source, with a limited filter in between. You need to profess that you can't, or you won't know everything yourself, but you need to try and inquire within whether something makes sense. If the world relied heavily on pristine subjective self-realization, religions would be devoid of objective fanaticism.

Our scriptures proclaim that our *Jeevan muktas* (liberated souls) demonstrate that objects and the objective world are nothing but reflections of our subjective nature (*Atman*). If our subjective nature is still, like pristine water, the reflection of the objects (the objective world) is crystal clear. When the subjective nature (*Atman*) is choppy and full of waves, a distorted reflection of the objective world appears.

The visuals below indicate the subjective (you) vs. objective (world) metaphor described. In the ultimate form of self-realization, the subject and the object unify.

My quest for *Guru* still continues organically, but it does not deter me from *Vichara* (self-inquiry), which is the only scientific, personal, and deeply subjective way of self-realization. I hope my book can inspire other, more capable minds to unravel the splendid beauty that *Vedanta* truly is!

Chapter 19

MEDITATION AND MEDITATIVE TECHNIQUES

All the Mukhya Upanishads and the Bhagavad Gita proclaim the importance of meditation as the primary means of stilling our mind, so we prepare ourselves for spiritual liberation. The *Vedanta, Yoga,* and *Sankhya* schools are all unified in this thesis of deep meditation as a path for spiritual liberation. Even non-theistic religions like Buddhism and Jainism unequivocally endorse deep meditation to reach the highest purpose in life.

The holiest book for Hindus, the *Bhagavad Gita* (song of God), dedicates an entire chapter (Chapter 6) to the yoga of meditation. A few gems and impactful quotes from Chapter 6 of the Bhagavad Gita are highlighted here and offer step-by-step practical advice to the spiritual seeker. Who better to listen to on how to meditate than Krishna, the Lord of the Universe, the Personal Godhead, or *Saguna Brahman*?

I have embedded my personal practices in each of the steps highlighted by this profound river of knowledge.

STEP 1: PREPARATION

"Those who eat too much or eat too little, who sleep too much or sleep too little, will not succeed in meditation. But those who are temperate in eating and sleeping, work, and recreation will come to the end of sorrow through meditation."

"A yogi should constantly concentrate his mind by sitting in a solitary place, alone, with mind and body controlled, free from expectations and from acquisition."

It is important to start your meditation either early in the morning when it's very calm or during sunset. I have found that early in the morning works better for me, but it may be perfectly reasonable to pick any time of that day that works to your schedule. It's best to avoid the first two hours after a big meal.

Some purists prefer to stick to one place (a sacred place) for meditation. Although it helps to have familiar surroundings with great energy and vitality, it is not always practical. I have found that it does not really matter as long as you can find a quiet place to be detached from this world for a bit.

"Holding the body, head, and neck erect and still, being steady, looking at the tip of his own nose, and not looking around."

I have personally found maintaining an erect spine when sitting easier by using either a meditation mat or sitting on any hard cushion. You have to be absolutely comfortable and be able to stay still for a long time. Make sure your sitting position brings you complete relaxation. It is generally not recommended to sit on a chair, a sofa, or a bed unless you have an injury that prevents you from sitting down. Beginners can use back support on a wall to maintain an erect spine position.

I have found it harder to keep my eyes open to see the tip of the nose. I keep my eyes closed, my head straight, and my gaze down, which feels very naturally peaceful to me. Meditation is a very subjective experience, and certain techniques may not work for all, but the image of Buddha and Swami Vivekananda in deep meditation always seems to have a lower gaze. This is depicted in the visuals below and has an uncanny resemblance to the meditation posture. The sitting position is very personal, and those who have advanced *hatha yoga* training prefer the lotus pose (padmasana), which may not be required for those not trained in advanced forms of physical yoga techniques. The key to posture is maintaining a comfortable position so your mind is not constantly worried about physical positions.

Meditation with lower gaze

STEP 2: FOCUS

"He should remain seated with a placid mind, free from fear, and with the mind fixed on Me (Krishna, Saguna Brahman, or personal God) by controlling it through concentration, having Me as the supreme goal."

I usually start with two to three minutes of *Pranayama* (breath control). *Pranayama* helps to still your mind and is reasonably simple to execute. You need to hold the left nostril and inhale through the right nostril for a deep count of twelve. Make sure you count that in your mind ever so softly. Then, hold the right nostril and exhale completely for a count of six through the left nostril. You should feel your lungs expand when you inhale and collapse when you exhale. Now repeat this by inhaling from the left nostril, continuing to hold the right nostril for twelve seconds, and then exhaling through the right nostril. This constitutes one cycle.

As you progress in your meditation, you can increase from twelve seconds to twenty-four seconds, and so on. Once you are done with *Pranayama,* you are ready for the next step.

STEP 3: CHOOSING THE OBJECT OF MEDITATION

This is again a very personal thing, and some amount of experimentation is required to find the perfect match for the individual spiritual seeker. Most people find it easier to meditate on nature, which is significantly larger and grander than themselves. Some examples are things from our universe: the effervescent sun, the shining moon, our unlimited cosmos, towering mountains, the calm sea, and the gentle breeze.

Most theistic religions propose meditation on the image of your *Ishta Devata* (favorite image of your personal God) or *Saguna Brahman*. In Hinduism, there can be various incarnations of Ishvara. This *Ishta Devata* should inspire selfless love and devotion in your heart. It always helps to have a picture of your *Ishta devata* in the room where you are meditating.

Monistic philosophy encourages seekers to meditate on the absolute or formless. This can be very abstract and is extremely hard for beginners. Other forms of monistic meditation include meditating on the sound and power of AUM, which signifies the entire universe. This form of meditation is more palpable with some practice and experience. Advaita meditation also includes meditating on the meaning of the four *Mahavakyas* (great sayings) from the Upanishads.

There are other forms of Advaitic meditation techniques that contemplate the real self by negation (*Neti, Neti*): "Not this, not this" and are not advisable unless instructed by trained teachers.

My meditation technique involves meditating on the *Ishta Devata*. This typically involves chanting *mantras* or *japas* (praise of the Lord). These can be *"Om Namah Shivaya,"* which is praising the Lord Shiva, one of the incarnations of *Ishvara,* or *Saguna Brahman*. The quintessential goal of meditation is inner focus and reducing the thoughts in your mind. Repeated mantras, or japa, with single-pointed focus toward *Ishta Devata* are one of the tried and tested ways to achieve this purpose. Breathing techniques while doing the *mantra,* or *japa,* are of paramount importance. An effective technique is to continuously repeat the following:

deep inhalation by silently chanting *Om*.

Hold the breath for one to two seconds.

deep exhalation by silently chanting *Namah Shivaya*.

For maximum gains, it's advisable to repeat the above mantra 108 times, or whatever number allows you to get into a continuous flow or rhythm to pour your heart's love and devotion to your *Ishta devata*.

One can also meditate on Lord Krishna, and the image of the supreme Lord as *Vishwa Roopa Darshana* (from Chapter 11 of the Bhagavad Gita) can also be effective. There are a few mantras that are a valuable tool while meditating on Lord Krishna.

"Om Namo Bhagavathe Vasu Devaya" or

"Hare Krishna Hare Krishna, Krishna Krishna Hare Hare."

It is critical to have a rhythmic breathing pattern while reciting these powerful *mantras,* or *japas.*

STEP 4: TURNING THE ATTENTION TO YOURSELF

Once you have established a single-pointed focus on the *Ishta devata,* your attention can slowly turn to yourself. These techniques are again very personal, and I have highlighted the technique that works for me. We discussed the concept of *"Sat-Chit-Ananda" as one of* the key attributes of Brahman (existence, consciousness, and bliss). Advaita Vedanta proclaims that this is the true nature of yourself.

An effective technique is to meditate on this nature of self.

Deep inhalation by silently chanting *Sat Chit*

Hold the breath for one to two seconds.

Deep exhalation by silently chanting *Ananda*

Visualize that you are nothing but unlimited bliss, and there is nothing but unlimited bliss around you. Inhale this unlimited bliss into your lungs and heart, hold it still, and exhale this blissfulness throughout your abdomen and the lower parts of the body. Feel this vivacious, blissful energy throughout your body.

There are guided mediation courses and spiritual gurus emphasizing a myriad of techniques to focus on the self. In essence, these techniques are truly 'subjective', and hence some amount of practice and patience are required to yield the desired results.

STEP 5: GRATITUDE

Once you have meditated upon yourself, I end with a brief acknowledgment of how grateful I am to be fully conscious and be able to meditate. How grateful I am to have what I have in my life: this universe, my family, the people around me, and the blessed nature of everything that surrounds me.

Meditation is not a quick-fix technique. Our minds are filled with endless thoughts that nest in and out. Holding the mind still and contemplating the true nature of yourself for at least a few minutes has an immense impact on the quality of your life.

As Krishna advises in the Bhagavad Gita, *"When meditation is mastered by concentration on the Self, the mind is unwavering like the flame of a lamp in a windless place."*

Like any skill in life, mastery requires practice, and meditation is no exception. Day in and day out, effort needs to be induced to practice meditation for at least 15 minutes, and ideally 30 minutes per session. You know you are really ingrained in meditation when you start yearning for it.

The Bhagavad Gita, Chapter 6, ends by highlighting the traits of a *Yogi*. (one who has mastered meditation)

"Supreme Bliss comes to this Yogi alone whose mind has become perfectly tranquil, whose defects and delusions have been eliminated, who has become identified with Brahman, and is taintless"

"One who has mind self-absorbed through Yoga, and who has the vision of sameness everywhere, see his Self, existing in everything , and everything in his Self."

Chapter 20

EMPHASIS ON PHYSICAL FITNESS

One might wonder what relevance, if any, the fitness of this impermanent body has to achieving spiritual liberation. The answer lies not in the end goal, but in the journey. The end goal is **not** to have a supremely fit and strong body, but to have the relentless self-discipline and mental strength to push your body to the limits of what it is capable of.

A stronger and fitter body creates a conducive environment for a stronger mind, and a stronger mind drives one to develop a stronger and fitter body. The two aspects are inseparable. Both the body and the mind need to be supremely fit to achieve spiritual liberation.

The *Maha Acharyas* of Vedanta, Adi Shankaracharya and Madhvacharya, traveled barefoot thousands of miles from the southernmost tip of India to the northernmost tip of India to establish monasteries and preach Vedanta. The physical fitness and mental disciplines of these *Acharyas* are unparalleled, even to date.

A stronger and fitter body does by no means imply spending endless time in gyms and running tracks. It only means, if the individual is conscious enough, to challenge the body and embrace the physical pain or discomfort that comes as a result. Vedanta proudly proclaims that self-restraint, self-discipline, constant practice, and non-attachment to results are keys to success.

Physical fitness has always been of paramount importance for me, and I do not have a specific goal in mind except to push your body and marvel at what a strong mind and willpower can do to your body. There is no end to physical fitness; the body needs to stay fit and alert till the last breath. Achieving this is not easy, and it takes intense discipline and mental strength, which are the hallmarks of all Yogis.

Diligent fitness training involving cardiovascular or resistance training has been shown to have many health benefits, including better heart health, an improved aging process, maintaining stronger bones, and enabling better cognitive health and judgment skills. In essence, this improved state of mind is fertile ground for spiritual progress through meditation and the other forms of yoga (Karma, *Bhakti, Raja,* and *Jnana*).

One doesn't need to be an elite athlete, run ultramarathons, climb Mt. Everest, or deadlift 500 pounds in their pursuit of physical fitness. They constantly need to challenge themselves and their bodies and make continual, moderate progress. The body is a beautiful machine that is willing to be chiseled by the strong hammer of the mind and the will. Even the elite athletes got there with intense and relentless training. There are no shortcuts, and the journey is way more important than the destination.

Self-discipline, self-restraint, and habituation are some of the key mental traits inherently developed in the journey to enduring physical fitness. These traits are universally developed and ingrained in your system and reach far beyond the health benefits of physical fitness.

As an example, it takes great self-discipline to go running on a cold day or workout when the whole world is watching a game or still lying on the couch. Little do we know that this trait is significantly impactful in every facet of life, from making the right lifestyle choices to staying supremely organized to staying committed to a career to being committed to family and relationships to numerous other situations where taking the 'easy way out' is not an option. The same self-discipline gets you to meditate daily, which gets you grounded to achieve that higher purpose.

It also takes great self-restraint to avoid eating junk foods, sugary drinks, or excessive alcoholic beverages—all necessary avoidances in pursuit of physical fitness. The same self-restraint smears into other walks of your life by helping to make pro-active decisions rather than reactive decisions, whether it's engaging in a heated or angry debate with your family or office co-worker, whether someone cuts in front of you in traffic, whether you are waiting in line for anything, and countless other shenanigans in life.

Habituation also bleeds into other aspects of our lives. Habituation creates actions without spending mental energy. Great habits result in great actions. As long as the actions have a healthy dose of challenge and skill, we will be in a state of FLOW as discussed earlier. This FLOW gives us a higher-level of happiness than positive emotions. Habituation helps us take our pets for walks diligently while enjoying nature and the solitude of your pets' company; it helps us clean our homes and surroundings; it helps us cook great food for family and friends; it helps us attend seminars and events that align with our purpose; and it makes us meet like-minded people.

The cautionary advice is not to be zealous in our pursuit of anything. The concept of moderation is absolutely key. Extremes in anything will not result in the desired action. Bhagavad Gita (Chapter 6.17) says,

yuktāhāra-vihārasya yukta-cheṣhṭasya karmasu
yukta-svapnāvabodhasya yogo bhavati duḥkha-hā

"For him who is moderate in food and recreation, moderate in exertion in all actions, moderate in sleep and wakefulness, yoga destroys all pain and suffering."

A stronger and fitter body, coupled with a strong mind, prepares you to follow the four paths of *yoga* to enjoy the bliss that is life.

Chapter 21

SOCIAL MEDIA & MEDIA CONSUMPTION

The information technology world we live in today is revolutionary! Information is at our fingertips, and we are in the 'instant gratification' world. We don't need to struggle for anything. We don't even need to get out of our cars to get groceries or coffee, and maybe someday we won't even need to drive a car if autonomous driving takes off.

Most political science researchers are unanimous in concluding that, "The technologies that 50 years ago we could only dream of in science fiction novels, which we then actually created with so much faith and hope in their power to unite us and make us freer, have been co-opted into tools of surveillance, behavioral manipulation, radicalization, and addiction.".

The rapid popularity of social media (Facebook, Instagram, YouTube, TikTok, etc.) and endless media content on Netflix and other streaming platforms has made billions of people addicted to their devices (smartphones, tablets, and computers). Addiction seems like an alarming word, but it's a reality. Thoughts of living without a phone even for a few hours send shivers and depressive thoughts to most adults and definitely to the younger generation.

Various studies over the years have linked excessive social media usage to depression, anxiety, loneliness, and other mental health issues. It is estimated that over 70% of US adults and over 95% of US teenagers and young adults are on social media. That is a staggering amount!

Blaming social media apps is not the answer. A sharp knife is a tool that is an absolute necessity in the kitchen to cut vegetables but can also be used as a weapon, causing injury to yourself or others. Social media apps are no different; they are tremendous tools if used judiciously and can cause harm to you and others if used callously. By exercising self-restraint, moderation, and awareness—all *Vedantic* concepts that we have discussed extensively—it is possible to maximize the effect of social media. It is completely possible that Swami Vivekananda's message would have resonated throughout the entire world instantaneously if social media apps existed in the late 19th century, and that would have been a great boon for humanity!

The fundamental issue that we gloss over in the research on excessive social media use is the question of why. Why do we compulsively act to endlessly browse on Instagram, TikTok, or Facebook, or binge-watch Netflix or other streaming media? The answer is uncomfortable and what Dr. Mihaly refers to as the "greatest waste of our leisurely time." Lack of a higher purpose in life and lack of mindful living lead to indulgence in passive activities that include mindlessly browsing social media. Lack of purpose in life creates a lack of goals, which creates a lack of self-discipline, which creates a lack of focus, which lets the mind wander into a state of bingeful consumption. This becomes a vicious circle that entraps most of humanity.

Is there a way out of this? Yes. Is it easy? No! We discussed the highly transient nature of happiness through instant sensual pleasures in the chapter on FLOW. The harder problem with enduring happiness is that it's not an instant feedback loop; it takes effort, discipline, dedication, and relentless belief in a higher purpose. The even harder problem in the realm of enduring happiness is the realization that there is **no end** to the goal; it is a continuum of life.

One of the most impactful examples of the pursuit of a maniacal goal is that of champion Olympic athletes. It takes four years of discipline, dedication, and self-restraint for these highest-caliber athletes to be the best in the world. What happens after you win and continue to win? We even read stories of celebrated Olympic athletes (Michael Phelps is one example) who go into depression and substance abuse after reaching the goal that they fought so hard to achieve.

Most of humanity falls into either the category of having a specific goal or having no goal at all. This is where purpose comes in as a continuum of goals and is far higher than yourself. In the case of *Vedanta*, the goal of every single human is liberation, or *Moksha,* or union with this very universe. The practical way to describe this goal is for humanity to lead a blissful life—a life that savors every moment and inspires others to do so. When this stage of liberation is reached, goals just become mere means to an endless blissful life.

Vedantic teachings already give us a playbook for leading a better life, which can effectively be deployed to lessen the harmful impact of social media.

Focus on creation rather than consumption. As stated in earlier chapters, creative activities that have a balance between challenge and skill create a deep flow, resulting in gratification that lasts longer. Some of the activities include taking a brisk walk, exercising, playing a board game with the family, reading a book, cleaning and organizing, helping out a friend, and volunteering with a selfless goal, among other things.

Focus on inner contemplation, or mindfulness. Strive to be constantly aware of your surroundings. As in the proverbial sense "smell the roses," watch the sky with its beautiful formations and marvel at God's creation; closely observe how the water boils when you are making tea; observe deeply your spouse's or your kid's eyes and expressions; and see how joyful your pet is to just be around you. Turning your inner focus on yourself will give you tremendous joy in the external world and make every moment blissful. You will naturally tend to move away from mindless activities, including endless social media and media consumption.

Focus on having a clear purpose in life that is larger than yourself. We have proven that the happiness obtained by pursuing your larger purpose is the highest ladder of happiness and is more enduring. If social media is used as a tool to aid in your higher purpose, you will feel a sense of joy rather than depression. As an example, if your purpose is self-realization, exploring a wealth of podcasts, YouTube videos, online books, and scholarly articles will inch you closer to your purpose. Remember that the purpose should be selfless and significantly larger than yourself.

Focus on self-restraint. Your external senses, guided by animal instincts, are always pouncing to project outward. Social media is highly opinionated and often promotes hate, greed, jealousy, violence, and sensual pleasures. Observe your emotions when you peruse this content, but don't act on it impulsively. Acknowledge that there are always many sides to a story and avoid reacting online. As is said in the *Bhagavad Gita,* maintain equanimity just like an ocean remains calm even with rivers flowing into it from everywhere.

Social media is a powerful tool that can be harnessed to aid your higher purpose. Moderation, inner focus, mindful living, self-restraint, and higher purpose are all tenets that catapult living to extraordinary living to unveil eternal bliss.

Chapter 22

WORK LIFE

On average, we spend 25–30% of our adult lives working. The majority of us work with a motive in mind: earn a living, pay bills, and raise family. For most of us, 'work' is a means to an undefined 'end'. We even define our identity around work. When asked the dreaded "what do you do?" question, even the most reticent of us respond with "I am a doctor," "I am an engineer," and "I am a lawyer." Work is such a quintessential part of our lives, but are we truly happy in 25–30% of our adult lives, which we define as work?

There are a myriad of theories to make work and joy synonymous.

Successful CEOs and philosophers have a utopian view of work equating to doing things you love. Steve Jobs (arguably the most impactful technology visionary) famously said, "Your work is going to fill a large part of your life, and the only way to be truly satisfied is to do what you believe is great work. And the only way to do great work is to love what you do." Mark Twain echoed a similar theme: "Find a job you enjoy doing, and you will never have to work a day in your life." It is of paramount importance to love your work; however, not all are blessed with being able to earn a living while loving what they do. For every doctor, engineer, and rocket scientist, there are folks toiling hard, working with dirt, dangerous chemicals, heavy loads, intense heat, or cold, who find the 'love what you do', very utopian and inauthentic in nature.

The Bhagavad Gita and Upanishads proclaim that joy at work can only be obtained through selfless work. It teaches individuals not to be overly attached to the fruits of their labor and instead to focus on their actions. However, in this ever-competitive goal-oriented world, workers find it hard to make progress on the proverbial 'career ladder' without being hawk-eyed at the results.

Modern social psychologists like Dr. Mihaly and Dr. Seligman advise that joy at work can only be accomplished through complete engagement and flow, involving harmonizing skill and challenge. In instances where the challenge is constant, as in the case of a factory assembly worker who does the same thing every day, FLOW is still possible with a willingness to continually improve the skills. As an example, the factory worker can continually improve by reducing the time it takes to finish the assembly. There could be several examples of mundane activities at work that can be made challenging by continually improving skills. Turning these constraints into opportunities for expressing freedom and creativity creates FLOW, bringing joy even in mundane work.

We can make our work more joyful if we

incorporate love for work,

selfless action-oriented mindset,

complete engagement to create flow while striving to constantly match skills and challenges,

incorporating mindfulness to eliminate distractions,

and finding a purpose.

Here are some guidelines for the modern worker (arguably geared more toward the skill-based workforce).

Can *you* really love your work?

The answer to this question lies inward. The inner focus that is needed for spiritual realization is exactly the same tenet that is needed in your workplace to really love what you do at work. The realization that there are several things beyond your control (your boss's behavior, company performance, external economic conditions, the behavior of your peers, etc.) is key to inner focus. This is *Vedanta* 101, which we have discussed extensively.

Once you have a deep inward focus, you begin to search for the meaning and purpose of work and, ideally, tie to that a higher purpose, one that is larger than yourself. Contemplate and reflect on why you are in this job and what the true meaning and purpose of this job are. You should be able to redefine the purpose of this work. According to a Yale research study, hospital custodians (who often deal with cleaning up bodily fluids from patients that leave most of us nauseated) found their job more satisfying after the purpose was re-defined to the 'human' element of helping someone in significant pain. It is impossible to find purpose in a custodial job if one does not redefine their purpose.

Redefining the purpose universally applies to work we consider menial to the sophisticated and technologically challenging. Aligning or redefining your purpose with a higher purpose is paramount. The paths of *yoga* for self-liberation serve as a great guidepost to redefine your purposes.

As an example, constantly learning and gaining knowledge at work appeals to the *Jnana* (knowledge) *Yogis* in us.

Love and devotion to a certain industry, profession, or facet of work appeal to the *Bhakti* (love, devotion) *Yogis* in us.

People empowerment and selfless service at work appeal to the *Karma* (action) *Yogis* in us.

Using signature strengths at your workplace (please refer to earlier sections to take the quiz on finding your signature strengths) can significantly enhance your love for the work. Dr. Seligman clearly highlighted research that signifies the use of signature strength for enduring happiness in all walks of life, including work.

FLOW at Work

One of the primary reasons for lack of work satisfaction, resulting in us being robbed of joy at the workplace, is the inability to maintain a steady focus, or FLOW (as defined by Dr. Mihaly), at the workplace. A state of flow needs us to be in total engagement at tasks that result in a total lack of self-consciousness in a deeply absorbed state. This flow state produces gratification, which is higher and more enduring than the happiness ladder. The result of this complete self-absorption is timelessness and selflessness, both of which are essential steps in a higher state of bliss.

For a task to produce flow, the skills and the challenge need to be optimally matched. We have discussed in previous chapters that an imbalance in either skill or challenge can lead to anxiety on one spectrum and utter boredom on the other. To strive for this critical balance, constantly seek work where the challenge keeps increasing, which brings in a need to develop new skills to meet the challenges. Most engineering and business organizations structure career growth in a way to stimulates the need for better skills. We also discussed plausible examples of creating flow by focusing on developing skills even in an environment that stifles challenges.

Look for a spectrum of anxiety and boredom in your workplace. If you are anxious, your challenge might be too high, and you need to upgrade your skills. If you are bored, you need a more daunting challenge. In today's organizations, communicating this to decision-makers is key. Only a person devoid of purpose continues unfettered in these extreme scenarios, which will result in utter dissatisfaction or a lack of happiness at work.

One of the clear rules to achieve flow is utter concentration or focus on the task. In today's distracted world, it is necessary to have a single-pointed focus. Mindfulness techniques come in very handy to maintain a razor-sharp focus on the task at hand.

Mindfulness at Work

Vedanta and *yoga* philosophy have defined what the West called mindfulness thousands of years ago. We discussed the concepts of *Dharana, Dhyana,* and *Samadhi* in the context of achieving spiritual liberation according to the *Yoga* philosophy. *Dharana* is defined as the intense single-pointed concentration toward an object or thought, and in the context of work, when translated to an activity, it becomes mindfulness. The term 'mindful' is an interesting juxtaposition, as being mindful requires the mind to be 'empty', devoid of past memory and future thoughts, only delving into the present.

Being 'mindful' or 'present' involves avoiding distractions and multi-tasking. In the book 'The One Thing," author Gary Keller demonstrates that extraordinary results are obtained by just focusing on one thing and having a narrow focus. This is akin to avoiding multi-tasking and focusing on one task at a time. The modern workforce today is bombarded with distractions, and remote work exacerbates this problem. The workforce of today tends to deal with multiple distractions by multi-tasking, leading to significant inefficiency and productivity loss.

It is all too easy for today's remote workforce to be on a 'Zoom' call while being completely disconnected or disengaged in the conversation. The so-called office productivity apps do their fair share of distractions with constant bombardment of chat messages, emails, calendar invites, and for the folks who make it to the office, a noisy co-worker or mindless meetings or shenanigans associated with the 'watercooler' talk. It would be a miracle if we got to 30% productivity, which means 70% of our productivity at the workplace is disappearing into the ether! This deserves to be fixed.

As the proverb says, "To do two things at once is to do neither." We have all fallen prey to the perils of multi-tasking, where 'busy' work gets in the way of 'productive work'. Here are some productivity tips to maintain mindfulness and single-pointed focus or be in the flow during work.

Avoid or eliminate mindless meetings

Work meetings, just like life, need a purpose, and if there's none, there is not another time waster in the work world. Meetings can fill one's calendar and make them feel 'busy' but definitely not 'productive'. Organizations that fill their days with meetings typically have no clue how this overload is killing productivity at work. Reserve meeting time to discuss something 1-on-1, ideally face-to-face or to discuss something that has a specific outcome. Never leave meetings hanging without a closure. Carefully pick people who need to contribute to your team. Avoid inviting passive listeners to meetings. Having an empty calendar is the greatest boon for effective work that can create flow.

Self-Discipline

Develop the habit of working on one thing at a time. Make a list (ideally in a paper journal or diary) and stick to the list, come what may. Develop self-discipline to start with the most important task of the day. Turn off or silence your devices (smartphones, smart watches) and close all windows on your computer screen except the one you are working on. There are impactful studies that have shown the need to not start your day by reading emails in your inbox. These studies indicate that checking emails first thing in the morning is a priority that is dictated by others rather than yourself. The first thing that happens is that you lose control of your day. Of course, the above is a sweeping generalization and may not apply to all, but it is still critical to not let the external world dictate your work priorities on a consistent basis.

Only the accomplished *Yogis* can continue single-pointed work without distraction. However, dedication and devotion to this self-discipline create habits, and this becomes exponentially less inertial as the day progresses. This deep sense of inner focus and mindfulness will help you achieve 80% of the results in 20% of the time, and better yet, the flow of engagement generates gratification, which results in enduring happiness or job satisfaction.

Big Goal/Purpose, Small Tasks

At first, the thought of having a big goal (purpose) and small tasks seems paradoxical, but it is pretty critical for sustained happiness at work. This works at the macrocosmic level for a company or at the microcosmic level for you in your workplace. We have realized that having a purpose that is greater than yourself (spiritual) is the highest ladder of sustained happiness. It's essential to compartmentalize the higher purpose in your workplace. As always, the paths of *yoga* serve as a lighthouse when we are looking for purpose. The hierarchy, or ladder, is depicted below.

Higher Purpose (spiritual guided by the paths of yoga)

Work Purpose (Guided by Different Paths of Yoga)

Work goals (the bigger the better)

Tasks: One at a time with single-pointed focus

Strive to bring *Jnana* (knowledge), *Karma* (selfless action), and *Bhakti* (devotion, love) as tenets into your work for purpose or meaning.

Perhaps your purpose at work is to constantly learn and gain knowledge.

Perhaps your purpose at work is to empower other co-workers and customers through selfless action.

Perhaps your purpose at work is unfettered devotion and love to a particular industry, technology, subject, or greater good of humanity through your work.

Once you have an iron-fisted grip on your purpose, rest is easy.

With strong self-discipline and a bigger work goal written, break down into small tasks with clear, tangible results that can be measured. Write down the task list and mindfully focus on one task at a time. Constantly reevaluate the priority of these tasks to your bigger work goals, but steadfastly focus on one task at a time.

As Peter Drucker said, "Efficiency is doing the thing right and Effectiveness is doing the right thing".

Using the techniques described in this chapter, the modern worker can strive for both efficiency and effectiveness while bringing enduring happiness to the place where we spend most of our adult lives, the workplace.

ABOUT THE AUTHOR

Harsha Rao is a Chief Operating Officer executive in the technology industry with over 20 years of experience. He has developed, mentored, and led various technology teams to success, ranging from big Fortune 500 companies to technology startups. He has a Master's in Electrical Engineering from the University of Texas and an Executive MBA from Harvard Business School. Harsha is also an avid fitness enthusiast. He enjoys working out, hiking, and spending mindful time with his family and his dog. He is married and lives with his wife and his teenage daughter in Austin, Texas.

REFERENCES

Vedas –

www.archive.org for all authentic Sanskrit to English translation of the four Vedas.

Upanishads –

Kathopanishad by Swami Chinmayananda

Prasnopanisad by Swami Chinmayananda

Taittiriya Upanishad by Swami Chinmayananda

Kenopanishad by Swami Chinmayananda

Mundakopanishad by Swami Chinmayananda

Mandukya Upanishad with Gaudapada's Karika by Swami Chinmayananda

Mandukya Upanishad – Translated by Swami Nikhilananda

Brihadaranyaka Upanishad by Swami Chinmayananda

Chandogya Upanishad by Swami Chinmayananda

Aitareya Upanishad by Swami Chinmayananda

Ishavasya Upanishad by Swami Chinmayananda

Patanjali's Yoga Sutras – Swami Vivekananda

Bhagavad Gita

Bhagavad Gita – Commentary by Shankaracharya – Translated by Swami Gambihrananda

Bhagavad Gita – Translated by Swami Prabhupada

Bhagavat Gita – The song of God, translation by Swami Prabhavananda and Christopher Isherwood

Neo Vedanta

The complete works – Swami Vivekananda

The complete book of Yoga – Swami Vivekananda

Autobiography of a Yogi – Paramahamsa Yogananda

Meditation & Spiritual Life – Swami Yatiswarananda

Self Unfoldment – Swami Chinmayananda

Inner Engineering – Sadhguru

The art of Light – Dayananda Saraswati

Modern Psychology

Authentic Happiness – Martin Seligman

Flow – Mihaly Csikszentmihalyi

The One Thing – Gary Keller and Jay Papasan

The Power of Now – Eckhart Tolle